Cheers f

"Merle Harmo[...] human being. Like [...] ent and riveting. It sho[...] a professor, of broadcasting—teaching America the definition of class."
—Curt Smith, Author
Voices of the Game, The Storytellers
and *Of Mikes and Men*

"Merle was sitting at the top of his profession for five decades and thus he sat in on some of the great stories in the sports world. Now he offers them to us in a rare collection of good laughs and great memories."
—Randy Galloway,
Dallas Morning News and WBAP-820

"Wonderful stuff from a truly special man and broadcaster whose talents have endured and carried him through the decades of a brilliant career behind the microphone. I am especially honored to have been the last baseball 'color man' to work side-by-side with Merle Harmon, one of the giants of our industry."
—Norm Hitzges,
KLIF-570 and ESPN

"Merle Harmon is a born storyteller. Now he brings his own colorful and insightful peek at the sports greats who have crossed his path, from Aaron to Namath and many more in 40-plus years of broadcasting. Enormously entertaining."
—Jim Reeves,
Fort Worth Star Telegram

Merle Harmon
STORIES

with Sam Blair

Copyright 1998 by Merle Harmon and Sam Blair.
This publication may not be reproduced, stored in a
retrieval system, or transmitted in whole or in part, in
any form by any means, electronic, mechanical, photo-
copying, recording, or otherwise without permission of
Merle Harmon and Sam Blair.

Library of Congress Catalog Card Number 98-091300

ISBN 0-963584-1-3

Published by Reid Productions, Inc.
2817 Shadow Drive West
Arlington, Texas 76006
Phone & FAX 817-640-1928

Cover Design by Larry Hinson,
Dallas Advertising Design
Dallas, Texas 75219

PHOTO CREDITS All photographs supplied
by Merle Harmon, Sam Blair, Jim Bradley and
New York Jets Football Club.

Printed in the United States of America by
Mennonite Press, Inc., Newton, Kansas 67114

INTRODUCTION

My friendship with Merle Harmon always has been a joy—bright as a new penny, comfortable as old shoes. There are lots of reasons for this but a truly special one is that he possesses something money can't buy. Class.

I sensed Merle had it when we first knew each other casually and professionally, meeting at sports events which Merle broadcast and I covered as a writer for *The Dallas Morning News*. Then my family and I moved from Dallas to Arlington in the summer of 1985 and we learned our new home came with a bonus. When Karen and I attended our first neighborhood association barbecue, there was Merle. He and his wife lived just a half-block up our street.

As neighbors, we came to know each other up close and personal. That's when I knew my first impression of Merle was right. And conversations with him were fun and enlightening. The more he talked about all the personalities and experiences from his professional life, the more we realized we wanted to collaborate on an anecdotal book. So, here you have *Merle Harmon Stories*.

There also are a couple of things I find

Merle Harmon and Sam Blair visit The Ballpark in Arlington, home of the Texas Rangers.

fascinating about Merle's personal story.

One is how two great memories from his boyhood led to major career successes years later.

The first involved Merle acquiring his dad's love for listening to St. Louis Cardinals games on the radio at home in Salem, Illinois, in the 1930's. "The announcer was named France Laux and he was my hero," Merle said. "This led to my creating a great pastime for myself when there was no Cardinal game on the radio. I would make up the game myself and do the play-by-play. That was when the broadcasting bug first bit me." Merle became a catcher on his high school baseball team and dreamed of playing for the Cardinals some day. But after rejections at two Cardinal tryout camps he sensed his future path would take him behind the microphone, not behind home plate.

The second involved Merle's annual train trips to St. Louis to see the Cardinals play once he was old enough to earn some money selling magazines door-to-door. He saved two dollars to make the trip and always used the last 25 cents to buy Cardinal souvenirs, which became the envy of every kid in his school. That experience eventually led to his founding Merle Harmon's Fan Fair, a national chain of retail stores specializing in the sale of officially licensed sports merchandise.

The other thing? Well, Merle definitely is true to his beliefs.

He knew the first time he saw freshman Jeanette Kinner at Graceland College that they had a future together. It happened in September 1946, when Merle had returned to the Iowa college for his sophomore year after Navy service in the Pacific late in World War II. "I was walking into the reception room of a women's residence hall with my cousin, Glen Henson, when I spotted her," Merle recalled. "I said, 'Glen, you see that girl over there? I'm going to marry her!'" Jeanette was unofficially engaged at the time ("I didn't have a ring, but we had an understanding.") but Merle soon won her heart. So soon that they were married on New Year's Eve. On Dec. 31, 1996, they were honored at a Golden Anniversary party given by their five children—Reid, Keith, Kyle, Bruce and Kara.

Merle is genuine in his feelings for his family, friends and church. His beliefs in the Reorganized

Church of Jesus Christ of Latter Day Saints run so deep that he is an RLDS evangelist, speaking frequently at church services and other inspirational gatherings. As you might assume, he is blessed with an extensive vocabulary—all of it clean.

So much so that after he told me the story of baseball commissioner Judge Kennesaw Mountain Landis saying "half-ass" when he called Cleveland Indians manager Lou Boudreau on the carpet, Merle suggested, "maybe we should change that to 'half-baked'."

I disagreed, pointing out that Judge Landis clearly meant to say "half-ass."

"OK, Sam," Merle said. "You're the writer."

Spoken like a true friend—and first-class collaborator.

—Sam Blair

To Jeanette

*A beautiful wife, a wonderful mother and
a real champion for putting up with me
while I ran across the country all those years*

CONTENTS

A Penny Postcard Worth A Fortune **13**
"Mr. Baseball" Enters the Booth **16**
The Unforgettable Jackie Robinson **21**
The Legendary Halsey Hall **25**
Catching the Jets, Courtesy of Cosell **28**
Sam DeLuca, My 'Super' Partner **34**
Uecker Ad-libbed in Any Language **37**
Merle Harmon's Broadcast
    Partners Through The Years **40**
The Right Place at the Right Time **45**
Vic Power and the Bullpen Car **48**
Mel Allen: One of A Kind **49**
These Guys Were A Real Gas **51**
Lou Boudreau, Kid Manager **54**
The Shooter **57**
The Man Who Signed Mickey Mantle **59**
Bryant Gumbel's Trivial Moments **65**
The Roger Maris I Knew **67**
A Hall of Fame Interview **77**
The Judge Overruled Boudreau's "Strategy" **81**
The Great Wahoo Caper **83**
O'Brien to O'Brien to O'Brien to O'Brien
    —Hey, Wait A Minute! **88**
Doing It Wherever You Are **91**

Martin Finds A Pitcher With Heart	92
I'm The Other Guy	94
Charley O. Loved Nicknames	98
Dean Smith's Double Legacy	100
Herb Score: Special to the Finish	102
Opening Day: Elation and Deflation	107
Making It Okie Dokie in Muskogee	109
John Wooden's Beloved Assistant Coach	114
The Fan Fair Story	116
Great Day? Not For Me	123
Seeing Double	125
How It All Began	127
Hondo Ate Like He Hit—Big	130
Gray Matter in the Wild Blue Yonder	133
The Impossible Dream	134
About The Authors	137

A Penny Postcard Worth A Fortune

It was late July in the summer of 1949, my rookie season as a professional baseball broadcaster. As the voice of the Topeka Owls of the Class C Western Association, I re-created the broadcast of all the road games except ones played in St. Joseph, Missouri, and Leavenworth, Kansas. I travelled with the team to those two towns and broadcast the games live since both were close to Topeka and it was cheaper to do the games live than re-create through a Western Union ticker report.

Cheap was the right word, too. I received the same meal money as the players, *one dollar per day*. I also received an astronomical allowance of three dollars per day for a hotel room.

I couldn't get an air-conditioned room for three dollars per day, even in 1949. Needless to say, I didn't get much sleep when I was on the road with the team during a torrid summer with temperatures hitting 100 degrees almost daily.

Topeka was in St. Joseph to play the Cardinals, a likely nickname for a team affiliated with the St. Louis Cardinals. The St. Joe Cardinals were led by a fiery little second baseman named Earl Weaver, who never made it to the major leagues as a player but became the Hall of Fame manager of the Baltimore Orioles. Earl drove in more than 100 runs for St. Joe that season, and he cherished that achievement the rest of his career in baseball.

Years later, when we both were in the majors, Earl would have me vouch for that fact when I might be in his dugout to interview him on my pre-game show. He would be in a friendly argument with some of his players about the year he drove in more than 100 runs. Of course, no one believed him and I would bail him out.

One night the Owls played a double-header in St. Joe and, sure enough, the temperature soared over 100 degrees. With little sleep and a splitting headache, my only salvation was a fast twin bill. In those days double-headers in the low minors were scheduled as seven-inning games. I was praying for swift play since I was a one-man crew—announcer, color man and engineer. The only break I got was during between-inning commercials, which usually were on recording back in Topeka. Fortunately, the restroom was close to the broadcast booth.

But Lady Luck was not on my side. The first game went extra innings and the second was a wild-scoring, error-infested contest with several passed balls and wild pitches thrown in for good measure. I was on the air for almost eight hours, including filling the time between games.

By the middle of the second game my head was exploding, I was soaked with sweat and I could barely talk above a whisper. It was my first year, right out of college, and I was full of enthusiasm for the game and the broadcasts. But I was really running out of gas in that second game and I felt I should give my listeners some explanation. So I offered a feeble excuse, like "I hope you will forgive me for not being able to go all out on the broadcast tonight. You know how it is when you have a bad headache." I thought some might think I was sampling one of our sponsors' beverages too often, as my predecessor had a tendency to do.

Feeling I had covered the situation properly, I finished the game.

Back home in Topeka a few days later, I received a postcard from a female listener with the following message: "We've enjoyed your broadcasts until now, but don't tell us your troubles. JUST BROADCAST THE GAME!"

I was crushed. How could anyone be so insensitive? There I was, feeling I was about to die with a terrible headache in a wild double-header and some listener criticized me for mentioning it.

But once I got over my hurt feelings, I thought about the real message on that postcard. Throughout my career, I have considered it the most important piece of mail I ever received.

That listener tuned in my broadcast that night to

be informed and entertained. Maybe that listener had had a tough day on her job, and maybe she had a headache like mine. Maybe that listener had just lost her job. Maybe she was confined to a hospital room or worse still, had recently lost a loved one. She may have tuned in my broadcast to get away from her troubles for a few hours, but instead heard me complaining about a headache.

From that day forward, I never complained on a broadcast how I was feeling, even if it was obvious I had a bad head cold or whatever. When I became a senior announcer on the broadcast team my rules were: never complain on the air about the weather, hot or cold; never complain about the facilities in the broadcast booth; never complain about the travel schedule, or the hotel accommodations; and never talk about personal problems. Just broadcast the game.

Unfortunately, the penny postcard I received from that lady did not include a return address. To this day, I would like to thank her for the most important piece of mail regarding my broadcast work I ever received.

"Mr. Baseball" Enters The Booth

I knew Bob Uecker had a strong baseball background when he became my Milwaukee Brewers broadcast partner in 1971. I also knew he had much more.

When Bob finished his major league playing career with the Atlanta Braves, he moved back to Milwaukee, his hometown, to become a special assignment scout with the Brewers in addition to representing the team on special public relations assignments. He already was fairly well known on the banquet circuit because of his quick wit and humor, a talent that had landed him on the Johnny Carson Tonight Show several times.

In the good ol' summertime in Milwaukee, Merle and Bob Uecker worked on their suntans while working Brewers games outside their County Stadium booth.

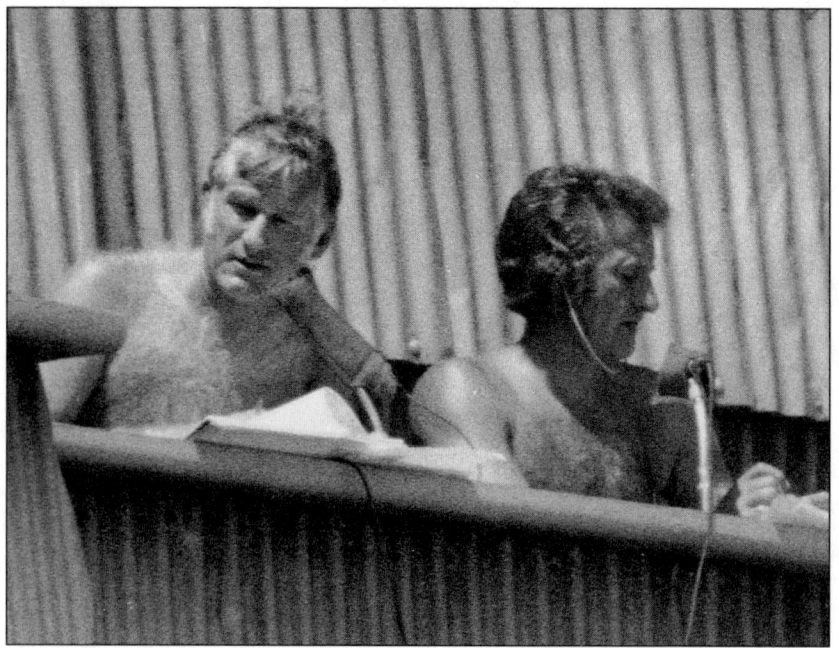

Bob had a large following throughout Wisconsin, so it was only natural that he would be tapped to join Tom Collins and me on the Brewers radio and TV broadcasts. The next year Collins moved into the ad agency front office and Bob became my full-time partner.

It was easy to see that Uke would become an outstanding baseball broadcaster. His reputation as a prankster and all-around funny man during his playing career did not diminish the fact that he was an extremely intelligent baseball man.

He was a fine catcher, with a strong throwing arm, and a good handler of pitchers. When I made reference to that on the air he would reply, "You're killing my reputation!"

Well, he did homer off Sandy Koufax—twice. Koufax probably is still trying to figure out how Uke did it. Uke's 14 career home runs and .200 lifetime batting average over six years earned him the title of "Mr. Baseball."

In 1974, after four years in Milwaukee, the Brewers had made little progress and decided to bring up their best prospects from the minor leagues. One of those prospects was an 18-year-old shortstop named Robin Yount. It was the start of the Brewers' climb to respectability and ultimate success. It also was the year that Merle and Bob hit their stride as a broadcast team.

It all began on a Brewer charter flight to New York early in the season. Someone got Bob started on some baseball stories and he had everyone laughing all the way to the Big Apple. The laughter continued on the bus from LaGuardia airport to the team's midtown hotel. Uke was still on a roll on the bus trip from the hotel to the stadium late that afternoon. By game time everyone was loose.

I always opened the broadcast by identifying where the game was being played and who the opposing pitchers were. Leading into the pre-game commercial I would simply say, "Bob will be back with the line-ups after this message." Coming out of the commercial I then would say, "Now here's Bob with the lineups." At which time he would give the same and I would start the play-by-play.

In previous games I had talked about Bob's speaking appearances at various functions and our listeners always had an interest in hearing the exploits of their hometown product. Milwukeeans loved the guy.

Anyway, I came out of the commercial that night and introduced Bob with, "Now here he is, just back from Capetown, South Africa, where he was the keynote speaker at the International Convention of Fake Diamond Cutters, Bob Uecker with the lineups for tonight's game."

Bob looked at me as if I had lost my mind but he didn't bat an eye.

"Capetown, South Africa," he said fondly. "I never thought this little old boy from Milwaukee would be invited to a place like that. As Merle said, I was there to address the Fake Diamond Cutters. I didn't even know those guys existed."

By now, I was thinking Bob was the one who was crazy. But he wasn't through. He went on to describe in minute detail the special instruments they used to cut the fake diamonds. He spoke with such authority he almost had me convinced those guys really existed. He wrapped up his dissertation in about forty-five seconds saying, "Yes, it was a great trip to South Africa but it sure is good to be back in the good old USA. Now here are the lineups."

I was flabbergasted. All I could think of was what our listeners, and especially Brewer owner Bud Selig, would say the next day. One thing for sure, they were going to think Harmon and Uecker should be confined in an institution. To make matters worse, the Brewers lost to the Yankees in extra innings.

I didn't have to wait long for a reaction. The first person I saw in the hotel lobby the next morning was Bud Selig. He had just flown in from Milwaukee and bemoaned the fact that the Brewers had played such a marvelous game but lost. Then he brightened.

"Say, you and Bob had a lot of fun before the game last night," Selig said. "I was driving to the airport in Milwaukee and I caught your act. I thought Uke was hilarious. You guys really were having fun. I hope you keep it up. Maybe it will carry over to our fans coming into our own ballpark. We want to provide our fans entertainment at our games just like you guys did on the broadcast last night."

I was speechless. Was he kidding me? Bob and I decided to find out.

Merle and Bob Uecker, decked out in tuxes for Milwaukee baseball banquet, also knew how to dress formal.

The next night, without telling Uke where he "had been", I struggled to think of something. Suddenly I remembered reading in the morning paper a story crediting Boyertown, Pennsylvania, as the casket manufacturing capital of the United States. So I said, "Now, just back from Boyertown, Pennsylvania, where he addressed the National Casket Manufacturing Association Convention, here's Bob Uecker with the lineups."

It was show time. "Boyertown, Pennsylvania," Uke started. "Boyertown is about thirty miles from Philadelphia and I was there many times when I was playing for the Phillies. As Merle said, I was there for the National Casket Manufacturers Convention and I was honored to be the starter for the famous casket races which are held as part of the convention. Those races are really terrific. They're similar to the Soap Box Derby. They put wheels on these caskets and line 'em up at the top of the hill on Main Street. Then they cut 'em loose and they roll down to the finish line. Since no power is allowed, the skill of the driver is very important. Of course, someone always has to cheat and this one guy put an 80-horsepower motor in his casket. Naturally, he quickly roared out in front of the others. By the time he passed Fourth Street he was clocking 60 miles per hour and raised up out of the casket to see where he was. Just then the town drunk staggered out of a bar. When the drunk saw the driver and the speeding casket zoom by . . . well, the guy has never taken another drink. Now, let's get to the lineups."

Bob's pre-game monologue continued on every broadcast for the next year and a half. They became so popular that fans flooded our mail boxes with suggestions where Bob would speak next. They even wrote scripts on how I would introduce Bob and what he would say. The fans really were having fun with us.

And the fans had so much fun when they came to County Stadium to watch the Brewers play that attendance soared from 600,000 the previous year to over one million. It wasn't long until the team became a pennant contender and attendance continued to climb.

I couldn't believe a couple of fans' reactions. Bob was on a radio talk show in Milwaukee and a lady called and told him she was recently divorced and discovered her ex-husband had given her a fake diamond. She asked Bob where she could find one of the fake diamond cutters he had talked about on that Brewers broadcast. Without hesitation, Uke responded, "Just check the Yellow Pages."

"Oh, thank you very much!" the lady replied gleefully and hung up.

I attended a party one night and a group of doctors were there. One respected physician came over to me and gave this advice. "Tell your friend Bob he'd better slow down. He can't be running all over the country and the world making speeches on his off days and between games. Nobody can go without sleep like that, not even doctors. Tell him to slow down or he'll be in my hospital."

I was astonished when I realized the doctor was really serious. It just proved that the key word in radio is "believability."

The Unforgettable Jackie Robinson

I never saw Jackie Robinson play in an official major league baseball game but I did broadcast a few of his spring training exhibition games. I never dreamed that some ten years later Jackie would become my partner on ABC-TV's Major League Baseball Game of the Week.

I met Jackie for the first time when we arrived in Boston to work our first game together in Fenway Park. The year was 1965 and I was in my second year as the voice of the Milwaukee Braves. I would do the Braves' Friday night game and then catch a red-eye flight to the site of the ABC game. Then when that game ended it was a mad dash back to the airport to rejoin the Braves wherever they were playing. Too bad the airlines didn't award frequent flyer miles then.

My first meeting with Jackie proved a most pleasant experience. I always had great respect for him as a ball player and for what he had done for the game and I had been told he was a terrific person and that I would enjoy working with him. That was okay, but what if he didn't enjoy working with me? He didn't know me from Adam and there was no doubt who the star attraction would be. My partner was the biggest name in baseball and it was apparent he would be the focal point of our telecast. Was he bigger than the game itself?

That question was answered in a hurry as Jackie and I walked out on the field in our ABC blazers to watch the Red Sox and their opponents take batting practice. The media swarmed all over Jackie. Flash bulbs popped. Cameras and microphones were shoved in his face. Writers with pens and pads in hand fired questions from every direction.

It made it easy for me to go about my business of

Jackie Robinson, right, brought his son, David, to one of his Major League Baseball Game of the Week assignments.

getting the lineups and some notes and quotes from the managers and players. Meanwhile, poor Jackie continued to be bombarded with questions. But he seemed to handle the situation as he had others: with total understanding and class.

Jackie did seemed relieved, however, when a production assistant pulled him away and told him it was time to tape our opening for the show, which would be played when we came on the air just before the start of the game.

I began to appreciate more and more that I was seeing true greatness in the person of Jackie Robinson. I thought I recognized it the first few minutes we were together at breakfast before that first game. He humbly sought the advice and help of everyone in our production crew.

"Don't be hesitant to correct me," Jackie said. "Let me know if I do anything off-base."

He was a hard-driving perfectionist as a player and he wanted to strive for the same kind of excellence as a television analyst. He was too proud to attempt to slide by on his name only. He wanted to do the job right in this strange new world, and was willing to pay the price of time and effort to learn.

No one had a better knowledge of the game of baseball than Jackie. And considering what he had gone through breaking the color line in baseball, no one had a better knowledge of life either.

On the field, Jackie was a win-the-game and take-no-prisoners type of player. But off the field, I found him to be kind, courteous, attentive, articulate, soft-spoken and a true gentleman.

How was Jackie Robinson as a broadcaster? The 1965 season turned out to be the only year ABC would do the Game of The Week and from the beginning to the end of the season Jackie improved steadily as he became more comfortable wearing a head-set microphone, listening to me in one ear and the producer in the truck in the other. If you don't think that can be distracting, try it some time.

As Jackie became more comfortable in the booth, his personality blossomed on the air. If he had something to say, he said it. He didn't just talk to hear himself talk, yet he made astute observations about what was happening on the field and what to look for in certain situations. Jackie also displayed a sense of humor on the air and offered hundreds of interesting tidbits about his own career, teammates and historic games he played in.

It was a shame ABC didn't continue the Game of The Week series. I would have loved working with Jackie for many more seasons. I did see him several times after that one season with him. When I was in New York on other assignments we would visit by phone or get together for lunch. He had a great concern for helping people advance in life, especially minorities. I'm sure that Jackie, as chairman of the board of The Freedom National Bank, did everything he could to fulfill the dreams of many.

In 1997, the 50th anniversary of Jackie Robinson breaking the color line in major league baseball, trivia experts searched for every possible note of special interest on Jackie. The day before baseball gave Jackie the supreme honor of retiring his number 42 forever, my friend Bob Ahrens, a New York television producer and trivia genius, called me. "Jackie Robinson also broke the color line as a major league baseball television analyst in 1965," he said. "Who was his broadcast partner on his first game?"

The answer: Merle Harmon. In more than 30 years, I had never given it a thought other than my fond memories of one of the truly great people I had the good fortune of knowing during all my years behind the mike.

The Legendary Halsey Hall

I met and worked with many characters during my 45 years in sports broadcasting. Most were loveable, a few were not. Halsey Hall definitely was loveable.

When I joined the Minnesota Twins broadcast team in 1967, Halsey and Herb Carneal were my partners. At age 70, Halsey still was going strong. He had enjoyed a long career as a sports writer for one of the Twin Cities newspapers and was a well-known football official in the Big Ten. He was in constant demand as an after-dinner speaker and had a huge following as a sportscaster and commentator on WCCO radio, which also was the flagship station for the Minnesota Twins Radio Network.

While Carneal and I shared play-by-play on both radio and television on the Twins' games, Halsey would tell little sidebar stories on players past and present and various games and events he had covered over the years. The fans loved it when we had rain delays and Halsey could hold court over the air. He was a legend in his own time in the Upper Midwest.

I had heard so much about Halsey I would have felt cheated if I had not had an opportunity to work with him. Funny things happened when you were around Halsey.

Like the time we were working a Sunday double header between the Twins and the White Sox on a hot July afternoon in Chicago. In the middle of the fifth inning of the second game, Carneal and I did our usual switch, Herb moving into the TV booth while I went over to radio with Halsey. Halsey was in the midst of giving scores of other games to the radio audience as he pulled them off the Western Union ticker tape. There were a lot of games that day and the floor was six inch-

Twins triple play of Herb Carneal, Merle and Halsey Hall had great fun calling the games for Minnesota fans.

es deep in ticker tape which Halsey had discarded after giving the scores. Halsey smoked more cigars than George Burns and as usual had one fired up.

I jokingly remarked on the air, "You know, Halsey, if you drop your lighted cigar on the floor, we could have quite a fire in the booth."

"Harmie, my boy," he replied, "never fear. I am always very careful with a good ten-cent cigar. I don't like to waste good money."

An inning later, I smelled smoke and I could feel heat around my feet. I looked behind my chair and all that discarded ticker tape was on fire. In the excitement of a Twins' rally, Halsey unknowingly had knocked his lighted cigar off the desk.

He quickly jumped out of his chair and tried to stomp the fire out with his feet, thereby creating a new dance step which, although unique, did not make it on "'American Bandstand."

While I continued to broadcast the game, I noticed that Halsey's sport coat, which was hanging on the back of his chair, had caught fire. The right sleeve was burning like paper.

Halsey grabbed the coat and slammed it against the wall a few times until the blaze was out. By then, help arrived and the fire on the floor also was extinguished. Remembering that "the show must go on," I never missed a play. Things returned to normal. Well, almost.

"Too bad about your sport coat, Halsey," I said.

"Don't worry about it, my boy," he replied. "I

wouldn't think about going on a two-week road trip without a spare jacket."

But Halsey couldn't let go of his fire-ravaged coat that easily.

The next night the Twins were in Baltimore to play the Orioles and I was down by the batting cage visiting with Brooks Robinson and some of his teammates when Halsey came up wearing a crisp shirt, colorful necktie, freshly pressed slacks and that BURNED-OUT SPORT COAT. The right sleeve was practically gone and the rest of the jacket badly charred. The players fell down laughing and 70-year-old Halsey revelled in the attention.

I commented on Halsey's attire during the broadcast that night and said he was "really fired up" for the occasion. Arno Goethel, the popular baseball beat writer for the *St. Paul Pioneer Press*, came up with the best line of all in his column the next day. He wrote, "Halsey Hall is the only man I know who can take an ordinary sport coat and make a BLAZER out of it."

When the Twins opened their next home stand almost two weeks later, Halsey found his mailbox filled with cards and letters commenting on his BLAZER. He loved them.

A few days later I received a telephone call from a lady whose husband was an executive with the 3M company, based in St. Paul and the developer of a material used in fire-fighters' suits and also used in the space program by the astronauts. You could hit that stuff with a blowtorch and it wouldn't burn.

This lady told me she had a gift for Halsey and asked if she could come up to our broadcast booth before the game that night and present it to him. I assured her she would be most welcome. Halsey always enjoyed receiving gifts from the fans—usually cookies, pies and cakes.

The lady arrived at the booth that night with a large, beautifully-wrapped package, presented it to Halsey and waited for his reaction. He hurriedly tore off the wrapping, opened the box and took out an impeccably hand-tailored jacket made from the shiny silver material used in the astronauts' space suits.

The enclosed card said, "Mr. Hall, this is one sport coat you never have to worry about being turned into a BLAZER."

Catching The Jets, Courtesy Of Cosell

In 1964 I became the radio and television announcer for the Milwaukee Braves. In addition to this assignment, the advertising agency I worked for also arranged for me to broadcast the University of Wisconsin football games and the basketball games of Marquette University where Al McGuire was taking over as head coach. I was thrilled by the opportunity to broadcast three such important venues.

I was quite contented as the month of June rolled around. Then I received a call from long-time friend Bill McPhail to begin a day that changed my broadcasting career. MacPhail was president of CBS Sports and his number one property was the National Football League telecasts.

"I've got a great deal for you," he said. "How would you like to be the voice of the Green Bay Packers on CBS?" I almost fell out of my chair. First the announcer for the Braves, a team loaded with stars like Hank Aaron, Warren Spahn and Eddie Mathews, and now the Packers, featuring Paul Hornung, Jim Taylor, Bart Starr and coached by Vince Lombardi. Wow! How lucky could I get?

MacPhail explained that the telecasts would be on a regional basis, which was the format in those days, and the job wouldn't pay all that well because the Packers were in a limited market, basically the state of Wisconsin. The money I didn't care about. To follow Ray Scott as the voice of the Packers would be the ultimate.

Then reality set in. I suddenly remembered I had made a commitment to do Wisconsin Badger football on a state radio network and since I had only been on the air with the Braves for such a short time I was sure

Howard Cosell had an opinion on everything, including how important it was to Merle's career that he broadcast New York Jets games.

the agency would never let me out of the Wisconsin games to do the Packers. So I told MacPhail I would have to turn down his offer.

All of this happened just prior to my heading for the airport to board the Braves' charter for a short trip to St. Louis, where they were to open a series with the Cardinals that night. My mind was clogged with disappointment during the flight as I wondered if I ever would have an opportunity to do network football again.

Those thoughts continued when we arrived at our hotel and I went up to my room to wait for my luggage to be delivered. I had not been there five minutes when the phone rang. A strange but highly-recognizable voice was on the other end of the line.

"Merle. Cosell. ABC radio has just bought the broadcast rights of the New York Jets and you're going to be the announcer. Get clearance on your schedule and I'll get back to you with details. Right now I'm a busy man." And with that he started to hang up.

"Howard!" I yelled. "Wait a minute. What are you talking about?"

"What I am talking about," he said, "is that you're getting the break of a lifetime. You're going to be the voice of the New York Jets, the team of the future in professional football. Now clear out your schedule and I'll get back to you."

"But, Howard," I protested, "I can't do the Jets games even if I wanted to. I'm under contract to do University of Wisconsin football this fall and just this morning I had to turn down an offer from Bill MacPhail to do the Packer games on CBS television."

"What?" Howard exploded. "Are you trying to tell me you'd compare doing the Green Bay Packer games with the opportunity to do the New York Jets on WABC radio, which covers the greatest market in the world! I'm talking about you working in the greatest city on the planet! The big time—the New York Jets owned by the dynamic David A. "Sonny" Werblin, the star-maker. The greatest impresario in the entertainment world! Are you telling me you would rather do the Packer games? How many stations do they have on their network—three? How many people do those stations cover anyway? Probably no more than you can put in brand new Shea Stadium, where you'll be working. Do you realize what I'm trying to do for you and what Sonny Werblin can do for you? Now get busy and clear schedule so we can lock this thing up. I don't have time to talk to you any longer. I'll call you back tomorrow. Goodbye."

After Cosell hung up, I sat stunned. What's going on? I'm offered the Packers in the morning and the Jets in the afternoon. But what's the use of thinking about it? The agency never will let me out of the Braves' games I would have to miss, and they surely won't let me out of the Wisconsin football schedule.

An hour went by before I got up the courage to call my boss in Milwaukee. I was shocked by his reaction.

"I think it would be a terrific break for you to become the voice of the Jets," he said. "I think it might be an advantage to have you exposed in the New York market. It possibly could help me when I hit Madison Avenue to seek additional sponsors for the Braves network. Do it. I'll get a replacement for you on the Wisconsin football broadcasts."

The next day I called Cosell to tell him I was his man. "You made a great decision, kid," he said in his distinctive nasal voice.

I really didn't know Howard well at the time he called me, and to this day I don't know why he picked me to do the Jets games. In fact, I don't know why ABC radio, through its flagship station WABC, wanted to do

Joe Namath's flashy style on and off the field helped fulfill Howard Cosell's prophecy that Merle would catch a winner with the Jets.

sports in the first place. WABC ruled the New York market in the ratings—out-distancing the other stations by miles with their Top 40 music format and all the best DJ's.

The only previous contact I had with Howard was an occasional "hello" when I was in New York doing sports shows for ABC television and he happened to pass me in the hall. But over time we became good friends and I can truly say no one ever treated me better when we worked together on the Jets games. Howard did the pre-game shows in his own style and brought a lot of credibility to our broadcasts.

My wife once asked me why Howard and I got along so well since we really didn't have a lot in common. He was a New Yorker born and bred with a law degree and, on a lot of occasions, a very sharp tongue. I was a product of the Midwest with a bit of a Missouri-Illinois twang. I finally came up with an answer. "I think Howard and I got along well because we had so little in common."

I was a play-by-play guy and he was a word-master. He could do sports reports and interviews like no I had ever heard before. As the sports director of ABC radio, he did a daily show for the network and, so help me, I never saw him use a script. I don't even think he could read a script. He would just scan the wire service reports, mentally locking in his mind the stories that interested him, then walk into the studio and do a flawless delivery. He was an absolute master at it.

A few years ago when Howard was terminally ill, I was in New York on business and called him at his apartment, where he lived alone since the death of his beloved wife, Emmy. I was told by mutual friends that he would not see anyone or take any phone calls, but I called him anyway. His nurse answered and I identified myself and told her if Howard didn't feel like taking the call just to tell him I was calling to express my friendship and appreciation to him. She told me to hold for a moment.

The next thing I heard was that voice: "Merle, my friend, how are you?"

For the next few minutes we reminisced and recalled that phone call I received from him that day in my St. Louis hotel room: "Merle. Cosell. ABC radio has just bought the broadcast rights of the New York Jets and you're going to be the announcer." I'll never forget his words.

A lot of good things happened to me in my career after that call and I'll always be indebted to Howard Cosell. Some may have been critical of the man who made Monday Night Football, but I could never be one of them.

Sam DeLuca, My 'Super' Partner

A severe knee injury ended an emerging all-pro career for New York Jets offensive lineman Sam DeLuca but he still made it to Super Bowl III. Sam was my broadcast partner as we called the Jets' dramatic win over the Baltimore Colts which changed the face of professional football forever. This was the game when the AFL champion first proved superior to the NFL champion and I'll always be proud that we were involved in describing it.

Sam DeLuca saw his fine football career ended by injuries but then pursued broadcasting the Jets with Merle with the same intensity.

DeLuca became the Jets radio analyst in 1968, my fifth season as play-by-play man. He was articulate, very bright and as meticulous in his broadcast preparation as he had been in the college classroom, where he had earned a master's degree in education. As a player, he definitely could remember the plays. As an analyst, he diagnosed the plays in a wonderfully clear fashion even a novice fan could understand.

Sam was a preparation freak. Before the first game we worked together, I walked into our broadcast booth at Shea Stadium and he already was there, poring over a half dozen hand-written pages of material he had gathered on the Jets and their opponents.

"I think I'm ready," he told me. "I have something on every player on both teams."

"That's great," I said, but my real thoughts were, "Boy, if he tries to cram all of that into the broadcast we're in for a disaster."

But that was not the time to offer a critique. It could wait until after the game, because I knew what was going to happen. The pace of the game would limit the amount of preparation he could use.

When the game was over, I told him, "Great job, Sam!" There was no doubt in my mind he was going to be a good one, a very good one, in fact.

But Sam was despondent. "I did a lousy job," he

Tight end Pete Lammons and quarterback Joe Namath were confident the Jets would win Super Bowl III when they appeared on "Jets Huddle" hosted by Merle on WOR-Channel 9 in New York. After the team arrived in Florida for final practices, Lammons said, "Don't show us any more film of the Colts. We'll get too optimistic!" Namath, speaking at a banquet, declared, "We'll beat the Colts. I guarantee it!" The Jets' 16-7 upset changed the face of pro football.

said. "I didn't get half the stuff I had prepared into the broadcast."

"That's why you did a great job, Sam," I told him. "You were 100 per cent prepared, but if you had used more than 10 per cent of your preparation you would have overwhelmed our listeners. You just never know which 10 per cent will be applicable to what happens during the game. If what you have fits, use it. If it doesn't, forget it. You did a great job."

Sam and I were together in the booth for the remainder of my nine years with the Jets. NBC Sports was so impressed with his work that they hired him away to become an analyst on their NFL Sunday telecasts and, needless to say, Sam always was prepared.

Uecker Ad-libbed In Any Language

Spring training 1971 was the start of nine great years with Bob Uecker as my partner on the Milwaukee Brewers' radio broadcasts. Bob is a talented, funny man who often surprised me with his knowledge. Like the day he told me he could speak Japanese.

Let me set the scene.

The Brewers trained in Tempe, Arizona, and, like most teams, they insisted on broadcasting all of their spring training games as a means of getting fans hyped for the season ahead. Of course, the announcers were supplied plenty of promos telling fans at home how exciting the team will be and to order tickets early.

That was easy to do. Announcers don't mind spending five to six weeks with their teams in Florida or Arizona. It's like a paid vacation. Golf in the morning, an afternoon game, a late afternoon by the pool

Merle teased Bob Uecker about making a comeback to attempt raising his lifetime .200 batting average.

and dinner in the best restaurants at night. All this and getting paid besides. What a life!

But once in awhile you do run into a bit of difficulty in broadcasting spring training games. Bob and I were having a great time in Arizona until I noticed that we were to broadcast the game between the Brewers and the Tokyo Lotte Orions the next day. This had to be a mistake. Although a Japanese team had trained in Arizona each spring for a number of years and played some major league clubs in exhibition games, no one ever broadcast those games.

I delayed reading the promotion spot for this game while our producer, Don Betts, called the advertising agency in Milwaukee which controlled our broadcasts to notify them of the mistake. The Brewers probably wouldn't even use any of their regular players and Brewer fans could care less about listening to a broadcast of the game.

The agency told Betts we had to broadcast the game. Although it was a mistake, the broadcast already was locked into the network schedule and we had no choice but to do it. So we started promoting the game between the Brewers and the Tokyo Lotte Orions.

The next day, March 18, 1971, was one of the most memorable in the annals of baseball broadcasting.

As I looked at the Lotte Orions roster and lineup with all those unpronounceable names I told Uecker, "Partner, we're in for it."

Bob just grinned. "We can handle it," he said.

"Not unless you speak Japanese," I replied.

"I do speak Japanese," he assured me.

"OK," I told him, "if you speak Japanese you do the lineups."

As customary, I opened the broadcast by welcoming our listeners: "It's another beautiful day in the Valley of the Sun, Tempe, Arizona, where the temperature is a dry 81 degrees and there's not a cloud in the sky. Today the Brewers take on one of the great teams of Japan, the Tokyo Lotte Orions. Now with the lineups, here's Bob Uecker."

"Thank you very much, Merle. It is a wonderful day for baseball and here are the lineups: Leading off for the Tokyo Lotte Orions will be Tom Toyota, center field; batting second, Nick Nissan, third base; No. 3 is

Sal Subaru, left field; and batting clean-up is Paul Panasonic, catcher..."

Startled, I interrupted Bob. "What are you doing?" I said on the air as I looked over and saw our producer panic-struck. "You told me you spoke Japanese and could handle those names."

Bob shrugged. "What difference does it make? Nobody knows who these guys are anyway, and our broadcast isn't being heard in Japan."

Then he rolled on: "Batting fifth, Hank Honda, right field; sixth, Mike Mitsubishi, shortstop..."

Although our broadcast was not being heard in Japan, the two announcers broadcasting the Lotte Orions games back to Tokyo were sitting alongside us in an open booth. They gave Bob and me weird looks while talking all the time into their microphones. I think they understood every word we said. They pointed to their heads and I believe they were saying, "Those two guys crazy. Sick in head."

By the way, Paul Panasonic had quite a day, hitting a three- run homer and belting a two-run double.

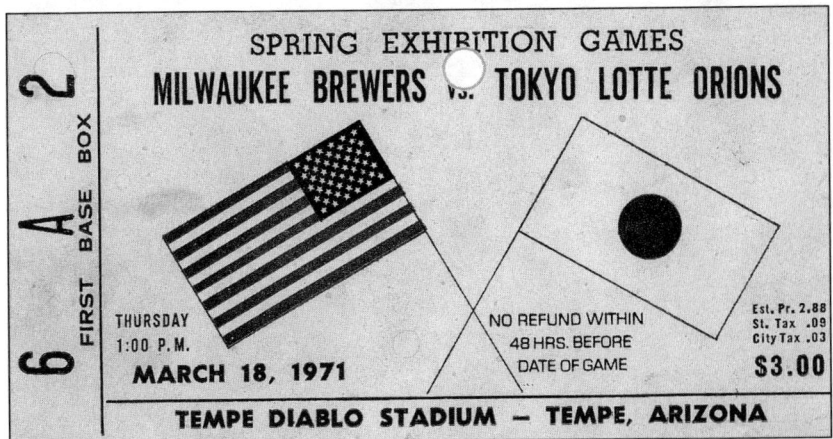

Three dollars bought you a seat to watch this rare international baseball exhibition, but Brewers fans back home probably had more fun listening to the broadcast.

Merle Harmon's Broadcast Partners Through The Years

Danny Abramowicz, New Orleans Saints, NFL, NBC.
Gary Bender, ABC and CBS, Big 10 basketball.
Gil Brandt, Dallas Cowboys VP-personnel, Univ. of
    North Texas football.
Frank Broyles, Arkansas AD-head football coach, NCAA
    football, ABC.

Al DeRogatis, a long-time headliner among NFL analysts, joined Merle on a number of NBC telecasts.

Otto Graham doubled as coach at the Coast Guard Academy while he teamed with Merle on the Jets radio network.

Dick Butkus, Chicago Bears, WFL, TVS.
Steve Busby, Kansas City Royals, Texas Rangers TV.
Herb Carneal, Minnesota Twins radio-TV.
Virgil Carter, Chicago Bears, WFL, TVS.
Jane Chastain, CBS.
Tom Collins, Milwaukee Braves and Brewers radio-TV.
Larry Conley, University of Kentucky, Raycom basketball.
Howard Cosell, ABC radio-TV.
Len Dawson, Kansas City Chiefs, NBC.
Joe Dean, LSU basketball, TVS.
Sam DeLuca, New York Jets, NBC, New York Jets radio.
Al DeRogatis, New York Giants, NBC.
Donna DeVerona, Olympic gold medal swimmer, TVS and ABC.
Dave Diles, ABC.
Leo Durocher, Dodgers and Giants manager, ABC.
Carl Eller, Minnesota Vikings, NBC.
Carl Erskine, Brooklyn Dodgers, ABC.
Forest Evashevski, Iowa AD-head football coach, ABC.

Otto Graham, Cleveland Browns, New York Jets radio.
Bill Grigsby, Kansas City A's baseball, Kansas City Chiefs football.
Lee Grosscup, New York Giants, ABC.
Halsey Hall, Minnesota Twins radio-TV.
Alex Hawkins, Baltimore Colts, CBS and TVS.
Norm Hitzges, KLIF radio, ESPN, Texas Rangers TV.
Mickey King Hogue, Olympic gold medal diver, NBC.
Paul Hornung, Green Bay Packers, TVS and NBC.
Hubert H. Humphrey, U.S. Vice President, ABC baseball.
Hot Rod Hundley, West Virginia basketball, TVS.
Jackie Jensen, NY Yankees, Boston Red Sox, Washington Senators, ABC.
Alex Karras, Detroit Lions, ABC and TVS.
Jim Kern, Cleveland Indians and Texas Rangers, Texas Rangers TV.
Kevin Kiley, New York Jets, Raycom.
George Kunz, Atlanta Falcons, NBC.
Jerry Lucas, Ohio State and NY Knicks, TVS.
Ron Luciano, American League umpire, NBC.

Bill Grigsby, a close friend since he and Merle broadcast minor league baseball in Joplin and Topeka, respectively, teamed on Kansas City Chiefs radio network.

Merle Harmon's Broadcast Partners Through The Years   43

Bruce Rice and Merle teamed on ABC's All Pro Scoreboard in 1961. Notice the "elaborate" set.

Gordon Maddox, Olympic gymnast, TVS.
Al McGuire, Marquette basketball coach, NBC.
Allie McGuire, Marquette basketball all-America, NBC.
Paul McGuire, LA-San Diego Chargers and Buffalo Bills, TVS and NBC.
Mike McCormack, NFL coach-GM, Kansas City Chiefs radio.
Minnesota Fats (Rudolf W. Wanderone Jr.), pool and billiards shark, NBC.
Joe Namath, New York Jets, NBC.
Bob Ortegel, Drake basketball coach, Dallas Mavericks TV, SWC basketball.
Billy Packer, NBC and CBS.
Bud Palmer, ABC.
Don Perkins, Dallas Cowboys, TVS.
George Plimpton, author and actor, TVS.
Larry Ray, Kansas City A's radio.

Burt Reynolds, actor, TVS.
Jackie Robinson, Brooklyn Dodgers, ABC.
Dave Rowe, Oakland-LA Raiders, Raycom.
Darrell Royal, Texas AD-head football coach, ABC.
Gayle Sayers, Chicago Bears, TVS.
Dan Spika, SWC supervisor of basketball officials, Raycom.
McLean Stevenson, actor, TVS.
Jim Sundberg, Texas Rangers-Milwaukee Brewers-Kansas City Royals-Chicago Cubs, Texas Rangers TV.
Fred Taylor, Ohio State basketball coach, TVS and NBC.
Gary Thompson, Iowa State basketball, TVS and NBC.
Frank Tripucka, Denver Broncos, New York Jets radio.
Jim Turner, New York Jets and Denver Broncos, NBC.
Bob Uecker, Milwaukee-Atlanta Braves, St. Louis Cardinals and Philadelphia Phillies, Milwaukee Brewers radio.
Bud Wilkinson, Oklahoma AD-head football coach, ABC and Raycom.
John Wooden, UCLA basketball coach, TVS and NBC.
Dick Young, *New York Daily News* columnist, New York Jets radio.

The Right Place At The Right Time

Like all young sports announcers, I dreamed of broadcasting major league baseball, but the odds of landing one of the premier play-by-play jobs were really slim in 1955. There were only 16 teams in the big leagues.

That meant there were only 32 to 40 jobs out there, since all but a few teams used two-man crews. The road to the majors for an announcer was similar to that of the ball player. You had to come up through the minor leagues and hope the right person would hear you—someone connected with one of the 16 big league clubs.

I served my apprenticeship broadcasting in Topeka, Kansas, in the Class C Western Association. Five years later, I was lucky enough to land a job announcing for the Kansas City Blues of the Triple A American Association. I thought I had the world by the tail. Kansas City was the top farm club of the New York Yankees, the finishing school for many of the Bronx Bombers' greatest stars. It couldn't get much better than that.

Our first baseman with the Blues was none other than Marvelous Marv Throneberry, who went to some notoriety with the early New York Mets. Believe it or not, Marv was a legitimate big league prospect when he was in the Yankee organization. But when he was picked up by the Mets he discovered he could make a lot more money being part of the buffoonery with Casey Stengel's shabby crew.

Shortly after the 1954 season ended rumors were flying that the Philadelphia A's were on the verge of bankruptcy. Kansas City was one of several cities trying to put together a group to purchase the club from legendary owner Connie Mack and move the team out of Philadelphia. In November, Chicago banker Arnold

Merle and broadcasting partner Larry Ray at the Kansas City A's first spring training. Ray was instrumental in launching Merle's major league career.

Johnson purchased the A's and announced that he would move the team to KC. I was elated until it dawned on me that I probably would be out of a job.

Like several hundred other guys, I hoped to be the new Kansas City A's broadcaster. But I was lucky to be in the right place at the right time.

Larry Ray, who brought me to Kansas City to be his partner on Blues broadcasts, was selected for one of the A's play-by-play jobs and then recommended me to be his partner. So in mid-February 1955 I signed a three-year contract paying me $10,000 per season. Thus began my 35 years of covering major league baseball.

I couldn't believe it. I got to see 154 games, plus spend six weeks in West Palm Beach, Florida. And I was paid $10,000 besides. What a life!

You can imagine what a dream world spring training was for a rookie announcer from the snowbound Midwest. Sunshine, the ocean beach, and dinners at fancy Palm Beach restaurants, all paid for by the A's network sponsor. Then every afternoon came the thrill of broadcasting games and talking about some of the baseball greats: Mickey Mantle, Ted Williams, Enos Slaughter, Allie Reynolds, Yogi Berra, George Kell, Ralph Kiner, Sandy Koufax, Robin Roberts, Don Drysdale and many others.

There also was a 20-year-old kid with the Detroit Tigers who had hit four homers in 1954, but word out of the Tiger camp in Lakeland was that he looked like a coming superstar. He proved to be just that. In 1955, he led the American League in hits with 200, slugged 27 homers, drove in 102 runs and won the league batting title with a .340 average. Al Kaline was the youngest American League batting champion ever. He also was a shoo-in for the Hall of Fame following a brilliant career.

I saw a lot of the Pittsburgh Pirates that first year in spring training. Like the A's, they weren't very good and both teams had problems scheduling the powerhouse crowd-pleasing teams like the Yankees, Red Sox, Phillies and Cardinals. The Pirates were loaded with kids, and they also had a young outfielder obtained from the Brooklyn Dodger organization who went on to lead the Pirates out of the National League basement and ultimately to a World Series championship over the Yankees in 1960. Roberto Clemente became one of baseball's great stars and also a great humanitarian.

At the height of his career, he was killed in a plane crash off the coast of his native Puerto Rico on New Year's Eve 1972. Clemente was a volunteer worker who was helping air-lift food and medical supplies to earthquake-torn Managua, Nicaragua. He was 37.

The Hall of Fame selection committee waived the mandatory five-year waiting period for candidates to become eligible for election and Clemente was enshrined in the Hall of Fame the year after his death. I am glad I was fortunate to see him play when he was so young and then follow his career for so long.

To this day, those budding superstars and famous veterans of spring training 1955 are vivid in my memory. I went to spring training 34 more years, but nothing ever will top that first one.

Vic Power And The Bullpen Car

In 1956, the Kansas City A's had probably the worst pitching staff in baseball, but they had the best bullpen car: a Lincoln convertible with a continental spare wheel kit on the trunk. The car was a bright magenta and looked a block long.

Every time the A's changed pitchers, which usually was several times a game, the bullpen gates in center field would swing open and a new relief pitcher would be chauffeured around the warning track and up to the A's first base dugout, where he would step out of his grand chariot and proceed to the mound. Then the convertible, which was furnished by a local dealer, would be driven back to its special parking place behind the center field gates.

The A's first baseman was Vic Power, a loveable Puerto Rican who was a fan favorite and one of the best glove men in the American League. Vic loved all the attention he could get, but it was that bullpen car that got *his* attention.

During each time-out for a pitching change, Vic would watch that convertible from the time it rolled out of the bullpen until it stopped to let the relief pitcher step out. He would walk over to the car for a closer look and fondly rub his hand on the hood.

Vic loved that car, and finally it got the best of him. After the season, he bought it! And he bragged that he got a good deal.

Well, maybe he did. That convertible made so many trips bringing in the A's relief pitchers the warranty had expired.

Mel Allen: One Of A Kind

Mel Allen gets my vote as the greatest sports broadcaster of all time. I may be a bit partial because he was such a special friend, but that's not an exclusive distinction. Mel became a special friend to anyone he met more than once.

I met Mel for the first time in 1955. He was the Voice of the New York Yankees and I was a rookie announcer for the Kansas City A's. I had never been to New York and I'll always remember my excitement looking out the window of the train and seeing the bright lights on the horizon as we approached the Big Apple.

The A's had just finished a series in Boston and were heading for three games with the Yankees. As the train pulled into Grand Central Station my heart was pounding with excitement . Oh, how I anticipated walking up the steps of the terminal and being caught up in the hustle and bustle of commuters heading for home, a scene I had seen many times in the movies. And it turned out to be just what I expected.

That was a memorable moment, but it couldn't compare with the excitement I felt the next day going to Yankee Stadium, not as a spectator but as a big league broadcaster! I was on Cloud Nine as I walked into The House That Ruth Built. This small-town boy from Southern Illinois had come a long way. Then, to make my life complete, I met Mel Allen.

I was getting settled into the visitors broadcast booth when Mel walked in, gave me a big smile and stuck out his hand. With that Alabama drawl and the most famous voice in sports, he said, "Merle, I'm Mel Allen. Welcome to Yankee Stadium. Glad to have you as a colleague. If there's anything I can help you with, just come right into our booth and ask. We sure want you to feel right at home, heah?"

I was so awed that I'm not sure what I said to him. Maybe I said, "How about that?" No, that was Mel's signature expression, one he used after calling a great play.

I never forgot my first meeting with Mel, and he was just as nice to me the second, third and fourth times we met. By then, I had learned he treated everyone the same way. His friendship was sincere, the kind you develop with a best friend.

Mel was not just the Voice of the Yankees, but the Voice of the World Series, the All-Star Game, the Rose Bowl and all the other great venues in sports. If it was big, Mel was at the microphone.

Special days for ball players were big, with lots of praise and gifts showered on the honoree. A new car usually was the top prize. The Yankees, with such legends as Babe Ruth and Joe DiMaggio, staged a number of these tributes but one of the two biggest days ever held in Yankee Stadium saluted Lou Gehrig. The other was for Mel Allen. More than 70,000 fans jammed the stadium to honor him and he drove away that day in a new Cadillac.

Those were the glory days for Mel Allen, and he deserved them. But in 1964, after 25 years as Voice of the Yankees, Mel was dropped by CBS, the new owner of the Yankees. The network didn't tell him he was not being renewed, but simply went out and hired someone else. To his dying day, Mel never received an explanation from CBS.

Mel was crushed. The Yankee pin-stripes were his life. He had no time for marriage, and little social life at all. He was devoted to the Yankees night and day—except when he took time out to be nice to people like me.

Fortunately, there still are plenty of us around who enjoyed that friendship. Mel Allen always will stand tall in our memories.

And somewhere I know Mel is smiling and saying, "How about that?"

These Guys Were A Real Gas

The heroes of my youth were the famed Gashouse Gang, a wild and wooly bunch of gifted baseball players who played for the St. Louis Cardinals in the 1930's and '40's and cut a wide swath through National League cities with their uproarious high jinx. They drove their managers crazy as well as their owner, Sam Breadon, who after each road trip usually received a bill for damages from hotels where his team stayed.

As a boy in Salem, Illinois, I would save my money to make my annual train trip to St. Louis to see these Cardinals play. They never disappointed me.

The Gashouse Gang was a bunch of fun-loving cut-ups who thought they were stealing when they received their paychecks, which might run as much as two hundred to four hundred dollars a month. Getting paid to play a kid's game? How could owners be so stupid?

Those Cardinals had some great nicknames. "Dizzy" Dean and his brother "Daffy," "Ducky" Medwick, "Pepper" Martin, "Hummin' Bird" Warnecke, "Frenchy" Bordagaray. They had their own musical organization of sorts. They called it "The Mudcat Band." They made some of their instruments and would entertain themselves on the long train trips between cities.

They also would crank up a tune or two in their dugout from time to time. The fans loved them and the opposition hated them. They would slide into bases spikes high or blast into a catcher in a close play at home plate. They were good and they knew it. They loved to sit on the top dugout step and razz the opposing pitcher or batter. They would fight at the drop of a hat—or brawl might be a better word.

When they went on the road they made themselves heard—on trains and busses, in hotel lobbies or the enemy ballpark. They didn't make much money, but there were plenty of laughs..

Mort and Walker Cooper formed one of the best brother batteries in the history of baseball. They led the Cardinals to three straight National League championships and one World Series title in the early '40's. Mort threw back-to-back 20-win seasons and Walker was a solid RBI man with a cannon for a throwing arm that kept the opposition cautious on the bases.

While Mort's career was cut short because of arm trouble, Walker had a solid 18-year major league career. As a kid, I envisioned myself succeeding Walker as the Cardinal catcher some day. When I saw a game in St. Louis I watched his every move. Then in my next game I tried to do everything the way I had seen the great Coop do it.

I became his friend in 1958 when he joined the Kansas City Athletics as a coach and I was the team's radio announcer. I couldn't wait for the team to take one of those long road trips to the East by train so I could corner Coop and have him tell me about the good old days with the Gashouse Gang. He never disappointed me. I would listen to his stories for hours.

He told a great one about the running war the Gashouse Gang had with a certain hotel manager in Cincinnati.

The low-budget Cardinals stayed in a lot of cheap hotels without air-conditioning and the one in Cincinnati certainly qualified. When the players' card games got a little loud late at night, the manager would call up and threaten to throw the team out on the street. Several times he came close to doing it, but the Gashouse Gang refused to back off.

One steaming summer night the temperature hovered around 100 degrees and the Cardinals couldn't sleep. Then one of them had a brilliant idea: everyone would fill their bathtubs with cold water, roll up in bed sheets and soak down in the tubs. Then, still wrapped in the dripping sheets like mummies, the players plopped down on their mattresses and fell asleep.

After the team left town the next morning the maids discovered the disaster. A few days later,

Cardinal owner Breadon received a bill from the hotel to cover the damages. He promptly deducted the amount from his players' salaries.

That didn't end the hostility, however. The Gashouse Gang decided to fix that hotel manager once and for all on their next trip to Cincinnati.

The morning after a night game, a group of players casually walked through the hotel in suits and ties, the required dress code in that era. They proceeded to a nearby paint store, where they purchased paint, brushes, drop-cloths, white overalls and shirts, a couple of step-ladders and some platform runners. They changed into their painters clothes and carried their supplies back to the hotel, pulling down their caps to cover their faces as they marched into the lobby and went to work.

They moved furniture away from the walls, spread drop-cloths over the carpet, set up their ladders and began painting a wall in the lobby. No one bothered them. The desk clerk and his assistants thought the hotel owner had ordered redecorating and were pleased to see it.

After working a half-hour or so, the "painters" took a break, walked out of the hotel, turned into an alley and changed back into their suits and ties. Then they walked calmly into the lobby and complimented the front desk staff on finally starting to redecorate the place. Two days later, the Cardinals left town and the hotel staff began to wonder when those painters would come back and finish the job. The hotel manager called his owner, who exploded when told what had happened. "Those crazy Cardinals!" he screamed. "They've gone too far this time. They're out of my hotel for good!"

You guessed it. Cardinal owner Breadon got another bill from the hotel and promptly deducted the damages from the players' paychecks.

"I think we forfeited most of our salaries that year," Walker Cooper said, "but we sure had a lot of fun."

Lou Boudreau, Kid Manager

Lou Boudreau was only 24 years old when he was named manager of the Cleveland Indians in 1942. And how did he get the job at such a young age?

Confidence!

Indians owner Alva Bradley had fired Roger Peckinpaugh after the 1941 season and was looking for a new manager. One day he called Boudreau into his office and asked the young shortstop who he thought would be a good manager for the Indians. Boudreau didn't hesitate. "Me," he replied.

Within a matter of minutes, he became the youngest manager in baseball history.

Lou was the playing manager of the Indians for the next eight years and led the Tribe to victory over the Boston Braves in the 1948 World Series. He later managed the Boston Red Sox, Kansas City A's and Chicago Cubs and in 1970 was elected to the Hall of Fame for all the right reasons.

Lou was a strong hitter, fielder and leader. And he was a swell innovator.

As manager of the Cleveland Indians, Boudreau tired of watching Ted Williams, a basic left-handed dead pull hitter, blast rocket shots through the right side of the infield. He challenged Williams by placing three infielders on the first base side of second, putting the shortstop where the second baseman would normally play, moving the second baseman halfway between first and second and back on the edge of the infield grass, and moving the first baseman closer to the first base foul line. That left the third baseman all alone on the left side of the infield and pulled over closer to second.

The maneuver became known as "the Williams

Harry "Suitcase" Simpson, Merle and Lou Boudreau in the early days of the Kansas City A's. By then, "Kid Manager" Boudreau was an elderly 37.

shift" and Ted never faced a Boudreau-managed team again without seeing it each time he came to the plate. Other managers liked the idea and also used it against Williams. Subsequently, other strong dead-pull hitters in both major leagues faced the defensive tactic originated by Boudreau.

There was more to this man's creative baseball mind. Lou also converted third baseman Bob Lemon into a Hall of Fame pitcher and created an outfield fence on wheels.

Cleveland Municipal Stadium, home of the Indians, was a massive oval structure seating upwards of 80,000. The distance down the foul lines was no more than 325 feet but the distance was so great in the power alleys and dead center field that it was almost impossible for a batter to reach the seats.

The Indians had a number of power hitters, but the New York Yankees, Detroit Tigers and Boston Red Sox had more. So Boudreau and the Indians decided to cut down the distances to the outfield seats against weak-hitting teams by erecting a fence from the left field to right field foul poles, creating reasonable distances for their long ball hitters and making the games more exciting for Cleveland fans. And they created even more excitement when they put the fence on wheels, allowing the ground crew to roll it back when the Yankees, Red Sox or Tigers came to town. Against teams like the St. Louis Browns and Philadelphia Athletics, the fence was rolled in closer again and the hard-hitting Indians had a picnic.

Boudreau got away with this caper for a few games until rival teams filed a complaint with the commissioner, Judge Kennesaw Mountain Landis. The tough old judge ruled the Indians must select one location for their rolling fence and leave it there for the remainder of the season. After that season the commissioner ruled that teams had the right to alter their outfield fences any way they wanted in the off-season but once a new season began they couldn't be moved.

The commissioner's order was called "The Boudreau Rule."

The Shooter

Chet Forte was one of the most talented sports television sports producers and directors I ever had the good fortune to work with. Chet built his career at ABC directing various network sports properties such as NBA basketball, NCAA football and the Olympic Games, but he really hit big as the man who called the shots in the production truck on the NFL's Monday Night Football show.

Forte loved basketball, though, and for good reason.

He made many all-America teams as a guard at Columbia University in 1955-57. As a senior, Chet was one of the nation's leading scorers, averaging 28.9 points per game when Wilt Chamberlain was tearing the nets apart for the University of Kansas Jayhawks. The interesting thing in comparing these two high scorers is that Chamberlain was a 7-footer and Forte stood only 5-9, which is probably stretching it some. Wilt was deadly at scoring around the basket while Chet was one of the greatest outside shooters of all time. He was a pure shooter in the truest sense, and he never lost his touch, even many years after his college career.

When Chet worked an NBA game he loved to go to the shoot-arounds (the workout teams have a few hours preceding their game that night) and challenge some of the NBA's greatest stars to a little shooting contest. The rule was, ten shots from the perimeter of the basket to see who would hit the most of the ten. To make things a little more interesting, a small wager was always welcome.

And so the challenge was on. The NBA star might hit six of his ten shots. Forte would hit eight or even nine and sometimes he was a perfect ten.

Away from the NBA, Chet gladly took on all comers. One night we were taping Marques Haynes and his Harlem Magicians in a game at Muskogee, Oklahoma, for Wide World of Sports. The Magicians were to play the Tulsa Oilers, a pick-up team made up of some pretty good former college players. Before the game, the Oilers noticed Forte out on the floor, all by himself, shooting a few buckets. One Oiler player sauntered over, mistaking Forte for some guy who just picked up a loose basketball and pumped up a few shots.

"Wanna shoot ten for a hundred dollars?" he asked.

Chet couldn't wait to pick up the challenge. "Ten shots for a thousand dollars," he answered. "None of this penny ante stuff!"

His challenger liked to have choked. "Man, I don't have that kind of money but I can go for a hundred," he said.

Forte relented and his opponent, who was the Oilers' best shooter, gave Chet the courtesy of shooting first. Bad mistake. Forte promptly sank nine out of nine and before he could go for ten, the guy stopped him. "OK, OK, I've seen enough," he said. He handed Chet a hundred-dollar bill and left the floor, muttering to himself, "Who is that little squirt anyway?"

He had learned, as Forte's old college opponents did, that Chet could knock down those long ones under pressure.

The Man Who Signed Mickey Mantle

I always loved the times I spent talking with baseball scouts of every level. Some scouted only major league teams and others beat the bushes, looking for talent at the grassroots level, including some kids still in their first year of high school. But all of them can tell you some great stories.

Some guys spend a lifetime signing raw young talent and never manage to produce a major leaguer, especially a major league star. Very few produce a bona fide superstar but those who do can be set for life as far as job security is concerned. I developed a lasting friendship with one super-scout named Tom Greenwade. He was the man who signed Mickey Mantle.

Tom was rather thin, weighing maybe 160 pounds, with slightly stooped shoulders. He walked and talked slowly with a pronounced "Missoura" drawl. You could tell if someone was born and raised in Southern Missouri. They pronounced the name of their state "Missoura." Tom definitely had the drawl and pace of Southern "Missoura."

I doubt Tom ever hurried except when he was driving his Cadillac, which always shone like it had just come out of a dealer's showroom. He had the face of a baseball scout: weather-beaten and somewhat wrinkled from countless days of sitting or standing in the hot sun and wind of farm yards and high school baseball fields across the Midwest. I don't think I ever saw him without the brim of his fedora pulled down to the top rim of his glasses, and he always had a slight squint as he eyeballed you during conversation or when he was watching a kid who hoped to catch his eye. Tom didn't scout for the money. He loved baseball and the thrill of

Mickey Mantle won the American League Triple Crown in 1956 with a .353 batting average, 52 home runs and 130 runs batted in.

signing and giving a kid a chance to fulfill every youngster's dream of becoming a big leaguer.

Not every baseball scout could afford to drive the backroads and city streets in a shiny Cadillac, but Tom could. He owned "Missoura" farm land and was a substantial shareholder in a bank in the town of Willard, population 2,177, near the Lake of the Ozarks.

Tom worked for the Yankees during their dynasty years following World War II when they were owned by Dan Topping, Del Webb and Larry MacPhail. The general manager was George Weiss, one of the toughest old birds in the business. Weiss ran a very tight ship and would not tolerate any player who didn't recognize the honor of wearing the Yankee pin-stripes. Weiss was a great believer in a strong farm system and his produced more talent than any other organization. Tom Greenwade was a star on his team of scouts.

One afternoon following a spring training game Tom and I sat in an empty stadium and he told me the story of how he scouted and later signed Mickey

Mantle. With that wonderful drawl, he spoke softly and slowly about his signing the young athlete who succeeded Joe DiMaggio, the famous Yankee Clipper who followed Babe Ruth and Lou Gehrig in Yankee lore. Yankee scouts for some time had scoured the country to find that special kid talent to follow the aging DiMaggio in center field and at bat, and Greenwade thought another kid in Oklahoma might be a candidate. His name was Jim Baumer. Every big league club had a pretty good book on this youngster who was tabbed "can't miss." Each was willing to spend a large amount of cash to get Baumer under contract.

Greenwade climbed in his Cadillac for the drive to Broken Arrow, Oklahoma, intent on signing Baumer for the Yankees, but he made a stop on the way which changed his career and made him one of the best-known scouts in baseball.

Tom had a little extra time so he decided to stop in Commerce, Oklahoma, and visit a family he knew, one which included a shy teenager who was playing for a semi-pro team in Baxter Springs, Kansas, just across the state line. Tom thought the kid was going to play for Baxter Springs that night but when he arrived at the Mutt Mantle home that afternoon he learned there were other plans for son Mickey. He was to graduate from Commerce High School that evening and his mother said there was no way he would skip commencement to play in a baseball game.

Mothers always win those kind of arguments, but this time there was a compromise. Mickey was all for playing baseball that night and his dad was, too. For years, Mutt always came home from a back-breaking day of work in the nearby mines and spent the remaining daylight hours teaching Mickey about his own passion, baseball. Tom said he and Mutt finally convinced Mickey's mother to let him play in the game once the early graduation ceremony ended. So Mickey collected his diploma, then headed for the game.

Tom said he and Mutt sat in the stands talking baseball when Mickey came to bat the first time. That's when the scout noticed something rather odd. Mickey, facing a right-handed pitcher, batted left-handed and promptly lined a sharp single to right field. Tom said he really didn't know much about Mickey, having seen him in one or two high school games during Mickey's junior year.

"Say, Mutt, I thought your boy was a right-handed batter," Tom said.

"I've been teaching him to switch-hit," Mutt said. "He's been doing it for some time now."

Tom saw Mickey drill another hit off the right-hander his next time up. Then the opposing team brought in a left-handed pitcher and Mickey went two-for-two batting right-handed. Mickey's performance intrigued Tom but he was not at this game to sign young Mantle. His interest was getting on down the road to try and sign Jim Baumer. He noted that Mickey stood about 5-11 and only weighed about 165 pounds. He had good speed but seemed likely to be more of a line drive hitter than a power threat. Mickey had a good throwing arm but was very erratic in the field at shortstop.

Still, something in Tom's mind told him that maybe it was worth spending another hour or so there and talk to Mickey and his dad about a future in the Yankee organization. It was the spring of 1949 and all major league organizations were looking for youngsters to fill out the rosters on their lowest minor league clubs. The Yankees had two such clubs within 50 miles of Commerce, Oklahoma—Independence, Kansas, in the Class D Kansas-Oklahoma-Missouri League and Joplin, Missouri, in the Class C Western Association.

Tom thought Mickey might play at the Class D level because of his speed and throwing arm and planned to pitch that idea to Mickey and his dad after the game. A rainstorm hit as the game ended, so all three of them scurried for the Mantle car. Tom and Mutt piled in the back seat and Mickey sat in front.

"You played a pretty good game tonight, son," Tom said. "Have you given any thought to playing professionally?"

Mickey was too shy to answer but his dad said, "That's all he ever talks about at home. He listens to all the St. Louis Cardinals broadcasts and envisions himself as being another Stan Musial. He worships the Cardinals."

Tom chuckled. "That's great, son, but I don't work for the Cardinals. Would you consider playing in the Yankee organization? I might be able to offer a fun summer job, playing baseball and getting paid for it, too. Are you interested?"

Mickey turned to Mutt. "What do you think, Dad?" he asked. "It's up to you, son," Mutt replied. "It's got to be your decision. You already have a summer job waiting in the mines."

Then Mutt asked Tom, "What kind of money could he make playing baseball this summer?" Tom rubbed his chin a few times, studying his answer. Finally, he said, "Oh, I think maybe I could get Mickey seventy-five or eighty dollars a month. That's a pretty good summer job for a 17-year-old."

Mutt was somewhat disturbed by the offer. "Tom, Mickey can make maybe twice that much working in the mines," he said.

Tom rubbed his chin again, then pulled out a pencil and started scribbling on the back of a used envelope. He knew the Yankees would not approve paying more than the Class D minimum for a kid they never heard of but there was something about Mickey he liked. He had speed and a good throwing arm but could he develop into a power hitter? The Yankees were looking for all three ingredients in the young prospects they signed. They also were searching for a future replacement for DiMaggio in center field but Tom wasn't thinking of Mickey in those terms. Mickey was a shortstop.

Finally, Tom quit scribbling on that envelope and came back with his best offer.

"Mickey, if I could get you $1,500 to play for the New York Yankee organization this summer would you sign with me tonight?" he asked. That got both Mantles' attention. While they thought about it, Tom wondered how he would get the Yankees to pay that much. He knew he couldn't but he was determined to sign this kid, even if he had to pay some of the money from his own pocket or add it to his expense account over the summer.

Mutt asked his son, "Mickey, do you want to play ball or do you want to work in the mines and stay close to home?" Tom quickly interrupted, "I'll arrange for him to play in Independence, Kansas, and that's only about an hour's drive from your home."

But Mutt had another problem. "Mickey's mother and I would be concerned about who we would be turning our son over to," he said.

Tom quickly satisfied him on that point. "Mickey

would be managed in Independence by Harry Craft, one of the truly outstanding gentlemen in baseball and a great teacher and motivator," he said. "He really looks after young players, just like a father."

Both Mantles were satisfied with that answer, so handshakes were exchanged and Mickey signed with the Yankees. But Tom never claimed he sensed that night that Mickey would become one of the game's greatest stars.

"I just lucked out," he told me. "I just took a slight detour on my way to see Jim Baumer, who eventually signed with the White Sox. I didn't even know Mickey was a switch-hitter. But sometimes it's better to be lucky than good."

But Tom and the Yankees did not know until Mickey's second pro season just how lucky they were. After an ordinary first year in Class D, Mickey moved up a notch to Joplin, Missouri, in the Western Association where he once again played for Harry Craft. By then he had muscled up to 185 pounds and started hitting baseballs out of sight. Craft decided that Mickey, with his speed and powerful throwing arm, should be moved to the outfield. Mickey was so impressive that the Yankees invited him to spring training with the major league club in 1951, less than two years after his high school graduation.

That spring Mickey hit some of the longest homers ever seen in a Yankee camp. He had been expected to return to the minors for more seasoning but when the Yankees broke camp manager Casey Stengel announced Mickey was going to New York. Mickey opened the season in right field, next to the great DiMaggio in center. At the end of the '51 season, DiMaggio retired and Mickey moved into his natural position, center field.

In 1950, when Mickey played for Joplin, I was a young announcer for the Topeka Owls, also a member of the Western Association. I never fancied myself a keen appraiser of baseball talent but I couldn't believe this kid's tremendous talent. The greatest mismatch I ever saw was Mickey's power against Class C pitching. I figured that Mickey would jump all the way to Triple A the next year.

But what did I know? Mickey went to Yankee Stadium instead.

Bryant Gumbel's Trivial Moments

When I was a member of the NBC Sports team I had the good fortune to develop a friendship with Bryant Gumbel, one of the truly great talents in the industry today. He was the greatest "winger" I ever met.

A winger is a person who can ad lib through any situation whether it be a sports event or a hurricane. When it comes to winging, Bryant has all the tools.

First, he's a very intelligent guy. He's well-read and can handle his end of a conversation on any subject whether on camera or over dinner. And his sense of timing is unbelievable. If the producer asked Bryant to fill for 17 seconds, that's exactly what he did. Not 18 seconds or 16 seconds—17 seconds right on the button. And nothing could rattle him. If you remember his work as lead anchor on NBC's Olympics coverage and as host of other major sports telecast, you know what I mean. Little wonder he became a huge success anchoring the Today Show for 15 years.

And Bryant prides himself in another strong suit: trivia. When I began working some assignments with him I quickly learned there was no one more serious about trivia than Bryant Gumbel. He was a trivia nut and it was almost impossible to trip him on any subject. Especially baseball.

But one Saturday when we were televising a game from Fenway Park, I got him.

When Bryant broke for the final commercial in his pre-game show, I asked him on the closed circuit, "Hey, Bryant, who's the only guy ever to play for the Boston Red Sox, the Boston Celtics and the Boston Bruins?"

"Gene Conley!" he immediately responded, then corrected himself. "No, wait a minute, Conley pitched for the Red Sox and played for the Celtics but he sure wasn't a hockey player so he couldn't have played for the Bruins. Now, don't tell me! I'll give you the answer when I get off the air."

When Bryant was back on the air for his final comments, I could see from the expression on his face on our monitor that while he talked he was thinking, "Who played for the Red Sox, the Celtics and the Bruins?" After the game, he struggled for the answer but finally gave up, a very rare occurrence with him.

"All right, who did play for the Red Sox, the Celtics and the Bruins?" he asked me. He waited with anticipation as I gave him the answer: "John Kiley, the *organist!*"

The expression on Bryant's face told me that I had better get out of town in a hurry. But then he broke into laughter and threw a few expletives my way.

That was the only time I ever tripped him on trivia. He was the best.

Some years later, my daughter-in-law Nancy called to tell me she was going to New York on business. She is a big fan of Bryant and the Today Show and she told me she would be walking by the show's set on the ground floor of the RCA Building on her way to an early appointment. She wondered what kind of sign she could hold up in the window that might get his attention. I chuckled in anticipation.

Her sign said, "Bryant, who's the only man ever to play for the Red Sox, Celtics and Bruins?" When he looked through the studio window and saw that sign he knew she was a Harmon.

During the news break he came to the window and greeted her. Nancy couldn't hear him through the glass but tried to read his lips. I told her later I could guess what Bryant was saying and I probably would be right.

The Roger Maris I Knew

When I saw Roger Maris play for the first time he was a rookie outfielder with the Cleveland Indians in 1957. He hit 14 home runs and drove in 51 runs that year and batted only .235, but there was something special about him. He came to play.

He ran out every ground ball and every pop-up. Roger had better-than-average speed and he was a terror running the bases. He took no prisoners when he broke up a double play and he had no fear about crashing into an outfield fence to make a catch.

I never could figure out why the Indians traded him to the Kansas City A's during the 1958 season. That year, playing in 51 games with the Indians and 99 more with Kansas City, he smashed 28 homers and drove in 80 runs. Maris never hit .300 in his major league career but his hits always seemed to drive in big runs. The Kansas City fans loved him. They looked upon him as their first legitimate star. Naturally, those fans were stunned beyond belief when the A's traded Maris to the New York Yankees after a year and a half. In 1961, his second year with the Yankees, Maris broke Babe Ruth's all-time record of 60 homers in a season when he connected for number 61 in the last game of the regular season. The New York baseball writers never forgave Maris for breaking Ruth's record and persuaded commissioner Ford Frick, a former baseball writer himself, to put an asterisk behind Maris' name because Roger played in 161 games—10 more than Ruth did in 1927.

But with the A's two years before all the headlines and controversy, Maris played one game against the Orioles that I'll never forget. It was a hot, steamy night, both teams were having terrible years and none of the players seemed interested in playing the game except Maris.

The general attitude seemed to be, "let's get this over with and then hit the streets," but Roger played it to the hilt. He drove in all the A's runs, three as I recall, and had an assist from the outfield with his great throwing arm. Of course, the A's lost.

I was sitting on the A's bus, waiting to go back to the hotel when several players straggled on, laughing and joking and making small talk. Then Maris came aboard. A teammate said, "Nice game, Rog."

"What do you mean, nice game," Maris shot back. The teammate said, "What are you so upset about? At least you had a good game." Maris exploded. "I don't care if I had a good game or not," he yelled. "WE LOST!" It was a silent bus all the way back to the hotel.

Roger never got the credit he deserved for being a team leader. He led by example rather than being a rah-rah guy. Traded to St. Louis after the 1966 season, his leadership was credited with driving the Cardinals to the pennant in 1968 despite limited playing time due to nagging injuries suffered challenging outfield fences over the years.

He deserves to be in the Hall of Fame. Others have made it with less credentials than his.

Merle did his first profession broadcasting in Trinidad, Colorado, in 1948 during his senior year at the University of Denver.

Merle, during one of his first broadcasts in Kansas City, was delighted to move up to calling games of the Triple A Kansas City Blues in 1954.

Merle, right front row, was honored as 1960 Sportscaster of the Year by Rockne Club of Kansas City. Green Bay's Vince Lombardi, third from right rear, was Pro Football Coach of the Year.

Merle took his new glamour job with the New York Jets in 1964 and team's program offered a photo to match.

Merle Harmon Stories   71

Merle goes "fishing" for a foul ball at Braves game in County Stadium in 1965.

Merle presents farewell appreciation awards to Braves stars Eddie Mathews and Hank Aaron at their final Milwaukee game in 1965. Club moved to Atlanta in '66.

Merle stayed busy with a variety of assignments for ABC Sports during the 1960's.

Merle relaxed beside the pool as he prepared for a Minnesota Twins' road game in 1969.

Merle, a familiar pre-game figure on the field in major league stadiums, prepared for an NBC Game of the Week in 1980.

Merle interviews BYU coach LaVell Edwards at banquet before the 1985 Kickoff Classic in Giants Stadium.

Merle became an elder in his church in the mid-80's and an evangelist in 1992. He speaks frequently at church meetings and motivational programs.

Merle enjoys a Kansas City reunion with the old Chiefs radio partner Bill Grigsby, Len Dawson and Kevin Harlan at Arrowhead Stadium in 1988.

Merle, doubling as Texas Rangers broadcaster and chairman of Fan Fair stores, throws the first pitch on Ball Night at Arlington Stadium in 1988.

Merle called his last baseball game on Texas Rangers TV network in September 1989.

Merle was inducted into Texas Baseball Hall of Fame in 1996 by fellow broadcaster and close friend Mark Holtz.

A Hall Of Fame Interview

Two of the most innovative managers I met in my 35 years broadcasting major league baseball were Lou Boudreau, who managed the Kansas City Athletics; and Bobby Bragan, skipper of the Milwaukee Braves. Fortunately, neither was reluctant to talk. Particularly Bragan.

I first met Bragan when he managed the Pittsburgh Pirates in 1956 and I soon realized he was a fantastic interview. Later, when we were together with the Milwaukee Braves, I hosted his pre-game show on the Braves' radio network. "Hosted" is a stretch, because all I had to do was turn on my tape recorder, introduce him to the radio audience and he took it from there. The next thing I said was, "Tune in before our next game for another Bobby Bragan Show." Sometimes I had to give Bobby the hurry-up sign to finish his three-minute commentary so we could get into the broadcast of the game itself. The show would go something like this:

"From County Stadium in Milwaukee, it's the Bobby Bragan Show. I'm sitting here in the dugout with the manager of the Braves. Bobby, what's the first thing that comes into your mind when I mention the name Branch Rickey?"

And Bragan would respond in that gravel voice of his . . . "Branch Rickey! Probably the greatest contributor ever to this game we play. Tell you what, fans, let's listen to the words of our fine sponsor and then I'll tell you all about Mr. Rickey."

After the commercial, Bragan would take over without my saying a word and begin telling a story that had even me enthralled.

He recalled the influence Rickey had on him when

Bobby came through the Brooklyn Dodger organization in the 1940's and later how Rickey hired him to manage the Pirates after he took over at Pittsburgh. Bobby told of his many conversations with his boss and the philosophy Rickey expounded. Like batting the team's best hitter in the lead-off spot and the second-best hitter in the number two position. His theory was that one or both would have an extra at-bat during each game and either one could come up with a critical hit to win a game. Bragan did just that when he managed the Pirates, often using Roberto Clemente, one of the all-time great hitters, in the lead-off spot and slugger Frank Thomas second.

Bragan then would recall a game where the strategy worked—Clemente, with two outs, came up that extra time and delivered a game-winning hit.

Then Bragan would tell why he occasionally inserted baseball's all-time home run king, Hank Aaron, in the Braves' lead-off spot. Same principle. An extra time at bat for the best hitter on the team.

"Well, Merle is telling me we're out of time and I

Felipe Alou, while not as talkative as Bobby Bragan, always brought a happy personality to Merle's interviews on Milwaukee Braves pre-game shows.

Bobby Bragan never was at a loss for words when he managed the Milwaukee Braves—nor has he been since.

didn't even get to tell you why I think Babe Ruth would have hit 65 home runs in one season if he had batted lead-off. But I tell you what. You come back and join me before the game tomorrow and I'll fill you in."

Sure enough, Bobby would pick up the next day where he left off the day before on why the Yankees should have had Ruth lead off. The way he figured it, the opposing pitcher never would have walked Ruth to start the game or when Ruth was the lead-off batter in any inning. Bragan figured Ruth would have batted an extra 33 times in the 154-game schedule, which teams played in Ruth's era, and subsequently would have hit an extra five or six home runs. He based that calculation on the fact that Ruth averaged a home run once every six times at bat.

Today Bragan is retired and living the good life in Fort Worth, Texas, and still believes in using your best hitter in the lead-off spot.

Bragan said, "If Brady Anderson hit 50 homers as the lead-off man for the Baltimore Orioles in 1996, how many do you think Babe Ruth would have hit in 1927, when he hit 60 batting third? I think any manager would like to start the first inning when his lead-off man gives him a run before anyone is out. Don't you think Davey Johnson (Orioles manager in 1996) knew what he had in Anderson? He wanted that quick run and Anderson gave it to him."

Branch Rickey's philosophy rubbed off on many players and managers, but none worshipped The Great Mahatma and expounded his principles more avidly than Bobby Bragan. Six decades later, Bragan's voice still is vibrant with admiration when he talks about the man.

The Judge Overruled Boudreau's "Strategy"

During World War II, hundreds of professional baseball players were serving in the armed forces. Consequently, many military bases fielded outstanding baseball teams. So on off-days during the season, major league teams would play the service teams on military bases as baseball's contribution to the war effort.

President Franklin D. Roosevelt determined that baseball should not be suspended during the war, as had been suggested by some, and that the game would be a morale booster for men and women in the military. Baseball Comissioner Judge Kennesaw Mountain Landis insisted the major league clubs use their first- line players in these games, treating them as they would any other game during the season.

The Cleveland Indians, managed by boy wonder Lou Boudreau, finished a weekend series against the White Sox in Chicago and bussed up to nearby Great Lakes Naval Training Center to play the base team Monday afternoon.

The Indians were contending in the American League pennant race and Boudreau, after using much of his pitching staff in the White Sox series and with a big series against the Yankees starting Tuesday in Cleveland, was in a dilemma. He didn't want to go against the commissioner's orders to use front-line players, including pitchers, yet he knew he had to rest his pitchers. He decided on some subtle strategy.

After one of his top hurlers worked the first three innings, Lou came in from shortstop to pitch and his pitcher moved to shortstop. The switch actually worked pretty well and all the sailors in the stands enjoyed watching Boudreau pitch. The game turned out to be rather competitive since Great Lakes Navy had several major leaguers on its roster. The Indians, pleased that they had helped boost morale, returned to Cleveland, but Boudreau found a telegram from Commissioner Landis waiting for him when he arrived home.

It ordered him to report to the commissioner's ofice in Chicago at 10 a.m. the next day or face suspension.

Needless to say, Boudreau made the meeting. As he was ushered into the commissioner's office, Judge Landis was seated at his desk looking down at some papers. He left Lou standing nervously before him.

Finally, Judge Landis looked up and said, "Mr. Boudreau, did you pitch in that game at Great Lakes yesterday and did you have a pitcher playing shortstop?"

"Yes, sir, I did," Lou replied.

"You, along with all other managers, were notified you were to play your regular lineup when playing service teams and you didn't do that," Judge Landis said. Then he fixed Boudreau with a hard stare.

"Mister," the commissioner growled, "I don't want any half-ass pitcher playing shortstop, and I don't want any half-ass shortstop pitching. Do you understand?"

"Yes, sir," Lou responded meekly, and was promptly dismissed by Judge Landis.

Boudreau never forgot that moment. "He made me come all the way back to Chicago for a five-minute meeting and didn't even ask me to sit down," he said. "What really hurt, though, was when he called me a half-ass shortstop."

Lou was entitled to take offense. He was considered the best shortstop in the American League at the time, and in 1970 was inducted into the Hall of Fame at Cooperstown, New York.

The Great Wahoo Caper

When I began broadcasting the New York Jets games in 1964, they were in their second year under the ownership of Sonny Werblin and his partners. The group had purchased the team out of bankruptcy court after the 1962 American Football League season when they were known as the Titans. Werblin was a great showman, so he was delighted to move his team into brand-new Shea Stadium in 1964.

The Jets were pretty bad but Werblin had entrusted the rebuilding process to his general manager and head coach, Weeb Ewbank. Ewbank had won two NFL titles as coach of the Baltimore Colts, where he developed a bunch of no-name players including Johnny Unitas, arguably the greatest pro quarterback of all time. Ewbank found himself in the same situation with the Jets and his roster changed rapidly as he searched the waiver wire each week for players cast off by other teams.

That's where Weeb found Edward "Wahoo" McDaniel, a linebacker who had been released by the Denver Broncos, the only AFL team worse than the Jets. Ewbank needed bodies so he signed McDaniel, a full-blooded Choctaw Indian who had played for Bud Wilkinson at Oklahoma in the late 1950's. Wilkinson's teams were so great that even a marginal player like McDaniel looked good surrounded by all that talent. And McDaniel's image was enhanced by his nickname. He had been called Wahoo since his high school days in Midland, Texas.

My broadcast partner with the Jets was Hall of Fame quarterback Otto Graham, who had led the Cleveland Browns to championship after championship first in the All America Football Conference in 1946-49

Wahoo McDaniel may have received more acclaim for making fewer tackles than any linebacker ever during his one season with the Jets.

and then, after a merger, in the NFL. Graham had a brilliant football mind and a great sense of humor.

As Otto and I discussed how to "sell" this shabby Jets team to a New York public that considered the Giants the only legitimate pro football team in town, we decided the Jets needed a hero who could catch on with the fans.

For years, one of the biggest Giant heroes was linebacker Sam Huff. Giant fans always loved how their defensive team played smash-mouth football. Chris Schenkel, one of the greatest sports announcers of all time, did the Giants games on television and constantly called Huff's name on tackles. Some critics said Schenkel made Huff all-pro but make no mistake about it, Huff could play.

So Otto and I went over the Jets roster again and again, looking for a potential Sam Huff we could turn into a hero. Otto kept saying, "These guys can't play. Most of them won't last the season. They'll get killed out there. Weeb, with Werblin's money, will put together a winner eventually, but it's going to be a real struggle."

I told Otto, "The Jets are moving into a beautiful new stadium and since the Giants games have been sold out for years over at Yankee Stadium, the Jets have an opportunity to pick up a whole new following. But they have to have a player become a household name like Huff did with the Giants. Let's just pick out a name, any name, that might catch on with Jets fans."

Suddenly I brightened. "Wahoo McDaniel!" I whooped. "He's our man! We're going to make him a household name in New York."

"But what if he's not playing?" Otto asked.

"Never mind," I said. "His name will carry him. I'll take care of that."

Knowing the Jets' fans didn't have much to look forward to in 1964, we decided to have some fun broadcasting the games. We didn't ridicule the team for its lack of talent and execution. Weeb and his coaching staff were giving it their best shot and some of those 1964 players like Dave Herman, Larry Granthan and Don Maynard went on to play on the Jets team that won the Super Bowl five years later. But Wahoo McDaniel was the Jets' most fascinating name in 1964. He was with the team only one year but every football fan in New York knew who he was.

The Jets' defense was on the field a lot that year because Joe Namath did not arrive until 1965 to ignite the offense. As bad as it was, that defense got lots of air time simply because the Jets' offense rarely had the ball.

I had two excellent spotters in Bob Ahrens and Artie Friedman and it was uncanny how accurate they were identifying the blockers and tacklers on each play. When the opponents ran a play, Bob would identify the ball carrier, passer or receiver immediately and Artie was just as quick on who made the stop for the defense. My call might go like this:

"Bills quarterback Jack Kemp hands off to his fullback, Cookie Gilchrist, who smashes his way for nine yards to the Jets 21-yard line." Friedman would point out that the tackle was made by the Jets' Ralph Baker and Gerry Philbin, but then I would say, "also in on that tackle was Wahoo McDaniel."

Artie would frantically shake his head—no, no, no!

But I would go on. "Wahoo is all over the place today."

On the next play I had Wahoo joining in on the tackle again. And the next and the next. When we came to a timeout, Bob and Artie both said, "You've got Wahoo in on plays when he isn't even in the game." "Don't worry about it," I told them. "I've got method in my madness."

As the season progressed, Wahoo played less and less but made more and more "tackles." Jets fans like to bring portable radios to the game and listen to the broadcast while they watched the game. It didn't take them long to figure out what was going on, and they began joining in the fun. After I would give proper credit to the real Jets tacklers, I would add, "and also in on that tackle was . . . guess who?" Otto Graham, turning away from his microphone, would cup his hands and yell, "Wahoo!" It was just natural that thousands of fans in the stadiium listening to us on their radios would yell in unison with Otto, "Wahoo!"

Until he found out what was going on between Otto, the fans and myself, Wahoo, from his seat on the bench, would look around the stadium with a startled expression, wondering, "Why are these people yelling at me? I didn't do anything." But soon he was in on the act. The fans loved it, Wahoo loved it, and even his teammates got a kick out of it.

Once, the Shea Stadium public address announcer, with his booming but sophisticated voice, said, "and that tackle was made by . . . guess who?" Two-thirds of the sellout crowd at Shea Stadium roared, "*WAHOO!*" McDaniel stood up from his customsary seat on the bench and took a big bow. The crowd went bananas. They loved him and his great sense of humor.

The next year Namath and company moved in as Weeb and his staff drafted high-quality players. With experience, that nucleus including Matt Snell, Emerson Boozer, George Sauer, Don Maynard, Al Atkinson, Dave Herman, Ralph Baker, John Schmitt and many others went on to win Super Bowl III in a shocking upset of the Colts. The Jets, led by Broadway Joe but without Wahoo McDaniel, became one of the most publicized teams in pro football.

And McDaniel, as Chief Wahoo, became one of the most publicized and popular professional wrestlers in the business, packing arenas wherever he performed. He reportedly has amassed a fortune as a wrestling promoter, but I'll bet he still treasures the phrase, "That tackle was made by . . . guess who?"

O'Brien To O'Brien To O'Brien To O'Brien— Hey, Wait A Minute!

In 1956, the worst team in major league baseball was the Kansas City Athletics. On second thought, the worst team was the Pittsburgh Pirates. Well, maybe they were identical twins in ineptness.

Although the A's finished sixth in the 8-team American League the previous season, they were destined to hit the bottom in 1956. The Pirates finished last in the National League in 1955 with Fred Haney as manager and they also were going nowhere the next season. In fact, both teams were so bad none of the other teams would play them in spring training exhibition games. Other clubs figured they would be better off playing minor league teams. So in the spring of '56 the A's, managed by Lou Boudeau, and the Pirates, led by new skipper Bobby Bragan, wound up playing each other most of the schedule in the Florida Grapefruit League. These two bedraggled teams even spent the last week of spring training barnstorming through the South on their way home for season openers.

General manager Branch Rickey had taken over the lowly Pirates and was in the process of building a powerful farm system, just as he did earlier with the St. Louis Cardinals and Brooklyn Dodgers. The Pirates led the world in signing kids fresh out of high school or college and force-feeding them through their farm system right up to the major league club. The only problem was that most of them were still years away from becoming bona fide major league players.

Oh, they had some interesting kids. Some were real

characters. They just weren't big leaguers. So Bragan, who was to become one of my best friends, always tried to make the game more interesting for the fans.

He was a great umpire-baiter and once pulled a sit-down strike on the field in protest of an ump's call. Once he even strolled out of the dugout with a bottle of orange juice in his hand, gave the ump a piece of his mind, then lay down on his back, propped one leg over a knee and started sipping orange juice through a straw. The umpire fumed while the crowd roared.

Naturally, Bobby was ejected from a lot of games, leaving his coaches to manage these pitiful Pirates for the rest of the day. But he always managed some satisfaction of getting back at the umpires. Maybe he pulled his best trick one day in Fort Myers, Florida, with identical-twin infielders Johnny and Eddie O'Brien.

The O'Briens came out of Seattle University as two of the greatest basketball and baseball players the school ever produced. They were only 5-foot-9 and 165 pounds but were so good in basketball they led Seattle to the third round of the 1953 NCAA Tournament. NBA scouts figured they weren't big enough to make it in pro basketball, but major league scouts sure liked their baseball talents. The Pirates paid both twins sizeable bonuses to sign with them but when they reported to the club no one could tell them apart.

When Bragan took over the Bucs in 1956, he never knew which one was Johnny the shortstop and which one was Eddie the second baseman. The Pirates, who desperately needed anything to grab the attention of their fans, hoped the handsome O'Brien twins would become fixtures in the middle of their infield and become drawing cards at the gate. Their flashy fielding was OK, but at the plate they had problems hitting major league pitching.

And so it was a hot, sunny March day in Florida that the Pirates were playing the A's—again. Johnny O'Brien, who wore number 6, played shortstop that day but Eddie O'Brien, who wore number 7, was not in the lineup. Around the sixth inning, Johnny was called out on strikes by the plate umpire and went into a rage. Bragan bolted out of the dugout to back up his shortstop and both wound up being thrown out of the game. To show you how bad the Pirates were to watch, it was one of the team's most exciting moments of the spring.

As Bragan and Johnny O'Brien marched off to the showers together, Bobby signalled Eddie to leave the dugout and join them in the clubhouse. Once inside the locker room, Bragan told Johnny to exchange uniform shirts with his brother and return to the dugout. At the end of the inning, the player wearing number 7 told the plate umpire he was replacing number 6 at shortstop for the Pirates. The umpire turned, looked up to the P.A. announcer and said, "Number 7, Eddie O'Brien, now playing shortstop for Pittsburgh."

Johnny finished the game and the umpire never knew the difference. Once more Bragan had won a battle with an umpire.

P.S.—Bobby pulled the same trick in several other exhibition games and always sat back and enjoyed a good laugh. But he swears he never pulled that trick in a regular-season game.

Doing It Wherever You Are

In 1980, NBC assigned me to cover the 70- and 90-meter ski jumps in the pre-Olympic trials at Lake Placid, New York. My job was to interview contestants just before each took off from the tower atop the mountain. The platform and warming house at the top of the tower were 257 feet above ground.

The little platform outside the warming house measured about four feet by four feet and was covered with snow and a heavy coat of ice which made traction pretty treacherous. If you slipped, a light railing about four feet high did not offer much protection.

As I stepped out on the platform with the contestant and his skis, there was no room to spare. In fact, it was so tight the cameraman had trouble framing the two of us in his shot.

Then I heard our producer, Terry Ewert, on my little ear plug that I wore to receive instructions from the production truck. "Merle, can you move back about a foot?" Terry asked. "We're having trouble getting the shot the way we want it."

I cautiously inched back and Terry kept telling me, "Just a little more, just a little more." Finally, he said, "You might try sitting up on the railing."

"Are you kidding?" I said. "The wind is howling up here and I'm having trouble just standing up. If I make one more move I'll probably fall over the side and it's 257 feet to the ground."

Terry was not impressed.

"Don't worry about it," he said. "If you fall, I'll have a camera on you all the way down and you'll be the lead story on the NBC nightly news."

Martin Finds A Pitcher With Heart

Billy Martin became a major league manager for the first time in 1969 when Minnesota owner Calvin Griffith handed him the reins of the Twins. Billy made an impressive debut.

That was the year major league baseball went to the divisional playoff system and Martin guided his team to 97 wins and the American League West title. The Twins' celebration was short-lived, however, when Baltimore swept three straight in a best-of-five playoff to advance to the World Series. But as the Twins broadcaster who followed the club from start to finish, my strongest memory is not of that playoff failure but the success of a patched-up pitching staff in the second half of the season.

Martin's staff was plagued with nagging injuries and the situation was made more difficult because Dean Chance, a 20-game winner two years earlier, was able to pitch only 88 innings all season. When Martin asked for volunteers to step into Chance's spot in the starting rotation, Bob Miller's hand immediately went up. Miller, a crusty veteran who had started only seven games in the previous five seasons, responded by winning five games in eleven starts. He was the leader of the charge down the stretch and one of his key victories was against the powerful Oakland A's in Metropolitan Stadium.

The game began at 11 a.m. on Saturday so as not to interfere with the University of Minnesota's opening football game that afternoon on the Gophers' campus 15 miles away. The morning start obviously agreed with Miller, though. Martin hoped Miller could hold the A's for five or six innings before he went to his strong bullpen. Surprisingly, Miller huffed and puffed his way through eight innings, silencing the A's bats while his offense built a 10-run lead. Martin planned to replace Miller at the start of the ninth but his determined starter wanted to pitch his first complete game of the season. Billy was concerned Miller might collapse after any pitch, but finally agreed to leave him in.

Miller retired the first batter but it was a struggle. The next batter was Reggie Jackson and Martin decided Miller had pitched long enough. "I thought his arm was going to fall off," Billy told me later.

As Martin walked out to the mound, Miller turned his back on his manager to indicate he had no intention of coming out of the game. Finally, Miller turned to face Martin and Billy asked, "Well, big boy, what do you want me to do?" "Get off the mound!" Miller barked.

Martin wheeled around and headed for the dugout, trying to contain his laughter. Just after Billy crossed the foul line, Miller served up his first pitch to Jackson. Martin didn't see Jackson smash the ball but he heard it. Crack! The blast resounded throughout the ballpark. Billy made a U-turn and headed right back to the mound as he watched Jackson's homer hit the batter's eye screen in dead center field 440 feet from home plate. "Give me the ball, you big turkey!" Martin told Miller. "I'm not taking the blame for you dying of a heart attack right in the middle of ballpark,"

Miller grinned, handed Martin the ball and walked off the field to a standing ovation. It was this kind of gutsy performance that won the hearts of Miller's teammates and the Twins fans.

I'm The Other Guy

To this day people will tell me, "I remember when you played at the University of Michigan, made all-America three years and won the Heisman Trophy. Yes, sir, you and that Forest Evashevski were really something. Evy was the greatest blocking back in college football history and you were the greatest runner. Harmon and Evashevski. I remember you well."

I also hear this from time to time: "Harmon of Michigan. My dad (or in some cases, granddad) told me all about you. He said you were the greatest."

Well, enough of that granddad stuff. I think I was in the ninth grade when Harmon won the Heisman Trophy in 1940 as he and Evashevski were driving Michigan down the glory road to championships and national headlines.

So why would Merle Harmon, a second-string end in high school and a junior college running back, ever be confused with the great Tom Harmon of Michigan?

Quite likely because when Tom retired from pro football with the Los Angeles Rams he became a West Coast sportscaster and eventually became a voice of college football on ABC television.

Merle Harmon—that's me—graduated from the University of Denver with a degree in radio broadcasting and, after working his way up the ladder, wound up working for ABC television in New York, doing college football games and the Prudential College Scoreboard each Saturday during the season. Both Harmons were affiliated with the same network so I guess it was only natural some people would think I was Tom. Tom was too nice a guy, though, to ever mention it to me. Others who knew there were two Harmons at ABC often asked me it Tom and I were related since we were about the same size and both us had gray hair and crooked noses. I'm guessing Tom got his the same way I got mine—

catching a linebacker's helmet in the face in the era before face-guards. But the similarities ended there. No, Tom and I were not related.

Still, I want to tell you a few things about Tom Harmon, Forest Evashevski and Merle Harmon and how our paths crossed occasionally, creating further confusion with sports fans.

My first exposure to network television was in 1961 when I became a free-lance announcer for ABC in New York, and that association lasted into the 1970's. I hosted Saturday Night Sports Final, the Prudential College Scoreboard following Saturday afternoon NCAA football telecasts, sat in for Chris Schenkel on a few NBA games and did occasional events on Wide World of Sports.

While I worked out of New York, Tom was based in LA for the network. Tom was the early voice of NCAA football and he was really good.

He did not become a professional broadcaster by accident. He once told me that he was planning on a career behind the mike while he still was a student at Michigan. He was a cinch to first have a career in the NFL but World War II interrupted. He spent more than three years as an Army Air Corps pilot and survived two plane crashes. Following the war, he played for the Rams and that led to his entering radio and TV in Los Angeles. He even starred in a movie, *Harmon of Michigan*. I liked it. After all, one Harmon should support another even if they weren't related.

So Tom became a headline sports announcer and here's the other guy, with the same last name and working on the same network, but who never was a three-time all-America, a Heisman Trophy winner, an Air Force pilot, a pro football player and a movie star. Me? Well, I enlisted in the Navy at age 17 in early 1944 and served on a troop landing craft in the South Pacific. I did work in a couple of movies but not one soul has ever mentioned seeing me in one.

Forest Evashevski played a role in my life quite different from the one he played in Tom's life.

Tom relied on Evy, a great blocking back, to diagnose the defenses Michigan went up against and then clear the way for another touchdown. Years later, as my partner on NCAA telecasts, Evy diagnosed what both teams were doing. He was a superb analyst and he made my job of calling the play-by-play easy. He was as meticulous in his preparation for our shows as he was preparing a game plan when he was head football coach at the University of Iowa, winning Big Ten championships and a Rose Bowl. Of all the wonderful analysts I have worked football with, Evy was one of my favorites.

I never will forget when Evy and I worked the Alabama-Mississippi game in Birmingham, not only because we watched the emergence of brilliant young Ole Miss quarterback Archie Manning but also because of a gala luncheon we attended there two days before the game.

Normally, our ABC crew would arrive at the game site on Friday morning. Evy and I would then spend the day with the coaches, watch both teams work out that afternoon, and attend the production meeting that evening. On Saturday afternoon we broadcast the game, then dashed to the airport to catch an evening flight. However, a week before this particular game, our producer in New York called and asked that Evy and I go to Birmingham on Thursday to attend a football luncheon and tell the fans there how we viewed the big game. This seemed a little unusual but we quickly agreed to be there.

Later we learned our producer called us after the network received an excited call from the program chairman for the Birmingham luncheon, asking if we could attend. He had just received a copy of a release from the ABC Sports publicity department about upcoming game assignments and saw the headline, HARMON AND EVASHEVSKI TO ANNOUNCE ALABAMA-OLE MISS GAME.

That Thursday Evy and I showed up at the hotel ballroom where the luncheon was to be held and took our places on the dais. When the program began, the master of ceremonies proudly announced, "Today we are honored to have with us two of the greatest names in college football history. At the University of Michigan they struck fear in the hearts of their opponents as they led the mighty Wolverines to victory after victory and in the process became an all-America tandem." Evy and I were stunned.

"This guy thinks I'm *Tom* Harmon," I told Evy.

"I'm getting outta here right now!"

Evy just grinned and said, "Relax, *Tom*. I'll cover you."

The well-meaning MC went on and on about Tom Harmon's great accomplishments and the audience was loving it. Finally, the moment came: "Ladies and gentlemen, let's have a big Birmingham welcome for Tom Harmon!"

What could I do? I nervously stood up, walked to the microphone and looked over at Evy, who was practically choking, trying not to fall on the floor laughing. I looked out at the audience, which was very generous with its applause, and noticed some rather inquisitive fans. They looked at the pictures of Evy and me in their program and then took a closer look at the guy standing at the microphone. I could almost read their whispers. "That must be him, Billy Joe, it says so right here in the program."

As the crowd quieted down, I decided, "Aw, what the heck, they'll never know the difference." But then I had a better thought: just turn the whole thing into a big gag by the luncheon committee which I agreed to participate in.

So I said, "Ladies and gentlemen, it is indeed a thrill to be here in the heart of Dixie where football is king. Without a doubt, you wonderful football fans are some of the most knowledgeable in America. That's why your program chairman and I decided to have a little fun today. Indeed, Harmon and Evashevski are delighted to be with you today and we will call the Alabama-Ole Miss game Saturday. But I ask you, who is this guy standing before you now? Is he Tom Harmon, the great Michigan all-America and Heisman Trophy winner? If you're saying 'yes', then the gag's on you. I'm the other guy."

The place erupted in wild laughter and applause. Then Evy and I told the usual football stories and the program chairman sighed with relief. Come to think of it, Evashevski and "the other guy" scored a touchdown that day.

Charley O. Loved Nicknames

Charles O. Finley, the flamboyant owner of the Kansas City-Oakland Athletics, thought there was more to baseball than just the game on the field. He decided the game and its players should be marketed just like any other consumer product. He wanted nicknames for his players, so he invented some dandies.

When he signed a player he would ask him if he had a nickname. If the answer was no, Charley O's fertile imagination quickly produced one.

When Jim Hunter signed with the A's he told Finley he didn't have a nickname. Finley thought a moment, then asked, "Do you like to fish?" Hunter grinned. "I love to fish!" he said. From then on the talented young pitcher was called "Catfish" Hunter.

Another pitcher, Johnny Lee Odom, joined the A's as a 19-year rookie and became "Blue Moon" Odom. One of Finley's theories was that the kid was so good he wouldn't lose once in a blue moon. First baseman Jim Gentile was called "Diamond Jim" because of his style of play. Shortstop Bert Campaneris became "Campy."

One nickname didn't pan out, however.

The A's had a rookie catcher named Jose Azcue at the time the Yankees' Yogi Berra was the top catcher in the American League. Finley ordered the Kansas City stadium announcer, Jack Layton, to announce Jose Azcue as "Yogi" Azcue. After one game of being called "Yogi" Azcue on the P.A. system, Jose was furious. He confronted Layton before the next game.

"You call me Yogi one more time and I'm going to climb right up the screen behind home plate and punch you in the nose," he warned Layton. The P.A. man never called Azcue Yogi again.

But you had to admire Finley's desire to make his team different from other clubs. He also introduced mustaches and beards to modern-day baseball in the 1970's. He offered each player $250 to grow a mustache, and he had plenty of takers.

Dean Smith's Double Legacy

In college basketball, there is a strong bond between the University of Kansas and the University of North Carolina even though the schools seldom have played each other. The tie is coaches—and one historic game.

Dr. Forrest C. "Phog" Allen was the first full-time basketball coach in America. He learned the game from its inventor, Dr. James Naismith, at . . . you guessed it, the University of Kansas. Now, let's fast-forward to the mid-1920's when a young Kansas farm boy named Adolph Rupp played for Allen at KU. Rupp, of course, went on to become the winningest coach in college basketball history at Kentucky. That record lasted for many years until North Carolina coach Dean Smith surpassed it in 1997.

And where do you think Smith played college basketball? That's right, the University of Kansas.

Smith was a substitute guard on Allen's 1952 NCAA champions and the 1953 NCAA runners-up, who lost the final game to Indiana by one point. In between, Smith also played on the gold medal U.S. Olympic team coached by Allen. That was a time in my life I will never forget. I was the radio voice of the KU basketball network.

So here's the lineup: Rupp and Smith played their college basketball at Kansas under coach Phog Allen, then went on to set national records for career wins at Kentucky (Rupp: 876) and North Carolina (Smith: 879).

And the story continues. Present Kansas coach Roy Williams, who played for Smith at North Carolina and later was his assistant there, has continued the winning tradition at KU. He succeeded Larry Brown, the vagabond coach of college and pro basketball who also played for Smith at North Carolina and led the Jawhawks to the 1988 NCAA title. When Smith retired in the fall of 1997, many figured Williams would return to North Carolina as his successor but Williams stayed at Kansas, where he has his own dynasty going.

Perhaps the greatest NCAA championship game ever was played at Kansas City in 1957 when North Carolina, a decided underdog, took on Kansas, led by the great Wilt Chamberlain. The game went to triple overtime before North Carolina finally won, 54-53.

Although the Tar Heels were ranked No. 1 nationally and the Jayhawks No. 2, Kansas was favored because of Chamberlain, a 7-foot sophomore scoring machine. Phog Allen recruited Chamberlain but he never had the opportunity to coach him. Allen reached the mandatory retirement age of 70 in 1956 and the Kansas Legislature refused to grant the popular and legendary coach a waiver. So Allen watched from the sidelines as his long-time assistant, Dick Harp, took over. Harp was under tremendous pressure to win it all, Allen having said that Kansas could win the NCAA title with Chamberlain and four cheerleaders.

North Carolina coach Frank McGuire took exception to that statement and devised a game plan to nullify Chamberlain's height advantage. His plan was to collapse his defense on Wilt and make the other Kansas players beat the Tar Heels. KU tried to adjust, but couldn't score enough. Chamberlain scored only 23 points, almost seven below his average, while the rest of the Jayhawks shot a combined nine-of-24 from the field. McGuire's assistant, who helped devise the winning defensive plan was that former KU guard, Dean Smith. A few years later, the young coach succeeded McGuire as North Carolina head coach and started his record winning career.

Now wouldn't it be ironic if present KU coach Williams, Smith's former player and assistant, ultimately breaks his old coach's record?

Herb Score: Special To The Finish

After 34 years in the broadcast booth of the Cleveland Indians, Herb Score has left the game to which he devoted most of his life. He was honored at the 1997 World Series when he walked to the mound for the third game to the Series—and the first to be played at Jacobs Field in Cleveland—to throw out the first ball.

He looked too young to be retiring when he wheeled that ceremonial first pitch down to the plate. It was hard to believe 43 years had passed since I first saw him pitch.

In 1954, I was broadcasting the games of the Kansas City Blues, then the American Association Triple A affiliate of the New York Yankees. The pitching phenom of the league was rangy 21-year-old lefthander Herb Score of the Indianapolis Indians, the top farm club of the Cleveland Indians. I couldn't believe my eyes when I watched his blazing fast ball and sharp-breaking curve. He was a little on the wild side—wild enough that opposing batters, especially those hitting from the left side of the plate, would just as soon take the night off when he was pitching. He clearly was destined for major league stardom.

The only reason Herb wasn't called up to the majors that year was because Cleveland was winning the American League pennant with a record 111 wins, breaking the stranglehold of the New York Yankees. The Indians were heavy favorites over the New York Giants in the World Series because they boasted the strongest pitching staff in baseball: Bob Lemon, Big Mike Garcia, Early Wynn, Bob Feller, Ray Narleski and Art Houtteman. There was no room for Herb Score.

This changed abruptly after the Giants swept the

Merle and Herb Score visit in 1958, a year after a critical eye injury halted Herb's journey to the Hall of Fame.

Indians in four games in the World Series. In 1955, Herb and I both went up to the majors: I as a broadcaster for the new Kansas City A's and Herb as one of the most exciting pitchers ever to put on a big league uniform.

Indians manager Al Lopez, one of the most respected managers in the game, was noted for developing great young pitchers. Cleveland general manager Hank Greenberg, the old Hall of Fame slugger, predicted that Lopez would turn Score into one of the greatest pitchers ever. Like fireballing Bob Feller and the great Lefty Grove, Herb could make hitters wilt in the batter's box.

Score was the talk of the American League as a rookie, winning 16 games and striking out 245 batters to lead the league. He was even better his second year when he won 20 games and fanned a league-leading 263. He averaged more than nine strikeouts per game his first two seasons.

Expectations were even higher in 1957 when Score pitched brilliantly in his early starts. But on May 7 tragedy struck in a game against the New York Yankees. A year later, Herb described it to me in detail in a pre-game interview.

Herb said he felt great that night as he went to the mound to face the Yankees. He was in control when the heavy-hitting Gil McDougald came to bat. There was no warning that his entire future, and even his life, would be changed within the next minute. Score rifled a fast ball to the plate and McDougald made solid contact. The ball exploded off Gil's bat and a white blur rocketed toward the mound.

Score said in the last split-second he saw the ball coming straight at him and tried to get his glove up to protect himself. But it was too late. The ball, which must have been travelling at more than 100 miles per hour, struck him flush in the right eye. Everything stopped. The big crowd fell silent as Herb crumpled on the ground. Trainers and doctors rushed to aid him, fearing the worst, that the blow might be fatal.

Herb remembered whispering as he collapsed on the field, "St. Jude, stay with me. Don't leave me now."

St. Jude is the patron saint of desperate situations. Jude also happens to be Herb Score's middle name. So he called upon his patron saint for help.

He said his mother taught him that praying when things are going well is just as important as seeking God's help in a crisis. He said he often prayed when he was pitching and that his teammates kidded him about it. But when the rocket off Gil McDougald's bat struck him squarely in the eye that night, those who had kidded him told him they were praying for him as he lay helpless on the mound. And the Yankees were praying for him, too. Would Score live? Would he lose the eye?

During all the trauma and suspense, Score still felt sympathy for a man he knew must be grieving over the accident. From his hospital bed, he sent a message to McDougald:

"Tell him that it's part of the game. It wasn't his fault. I don't hold any grudge or ill feeling at all."

But McDougald, one of the game's bright stars, never was the same. The sting seemed to be gone from his bat. He played three more years and retired at the age of 32.

Score had survived brushes with death before and that deepened his faith. When he was three years old, a truck hit him and nearly crushed both of his legs above the knees. The accident was followed by pneumonia. Then he broke an ankle and had a bout with rheumatic fever. When he was pitching his way through the minor leagues, he fell and dislocated the collarbone in his pitching shoulder. But nothing could compare with this tragedy.

Score spent three weeks in a Cleveland hospital as doctors fought to save his vision. They were successful, but he did not pitch again that season. He tried to come back in 1958 but won only two games in 12 starts. In 1959, he won 9 and lost 11.

His old manager, Al Lopez, had moved on to manage the Chicago White Sox and figured what Score needed was a change of scenery—a new city and new environment. Herb was traded to the White Sox in 1960, but it didn't help. He won a total of six games his first two years. He retired in 1962, a season in which he appeared in just four games and pitched a total of six innings.

Herb moved back to Cleveland, became an Indians broadcaster and developed into a solid professional for the next 34 years. The franchise deteriorated badly and during most of Herb's time in the booth crowds were so sparse in giant Municipal Stadium that Herb could almost count the attendance without missing a play. But he never lost his enthusiasm to be in the ballpark and he always was a welcome voice in the homes of the Indian faithful.

St. Jude must have whispered to civic leaders that Herb Score was special and deserved to broadcast a winning team. The Indians got new owners who poured millions of dollars into player development. The city built a showplace stadium and Indian fans started packing Jacobs Field the day it opened. Every game there has been sold out since.

And the team has been as impressive as its new home. The Indians have played in two World Series and either won the American League pennant or been in the divisional playoffs.

The 1997 World Series between the Indians and the Florida Marlins went the full seven games and the finale was a nail-biter—the Marlins finally winning, 3-2, in extra innings. In the ninth inning, the Indians had a 2-1 lead and were two outs away from putting a world championship ring on Herb Score's finger as he worked his final broadcast, but it slipped away.

Had Herb not been struck in the eye with the screaming line drive on May 7, 1957, he might have pitched the Indians to several World Series titles. Now he once again was denied something very rare and special. But he left the booth for the last time with a knowing smile.

For Herb Score, what might have been somehow was not meant to be.

Opening Day: Elation And Deflation

In baseball, Opening Day is always special, particularly if your team wins.

In 1967, Opening Day for me with the Minnesota Twins was one I'll never forget. New city, new team, new broadcast partners, new atmosphere. It was a great day in Minnesota, sunny and mild with the temperature in the 50's, a big crowd at Metropolitan Stadium and an exciting ball game which the Twins won.

I had just completed my first broadcast of a new season with my new team after two years in the National League with the Braves. I was really impressed with the friendliness of the Minnesota fans and their loyalty to their team. Hopes were high for an outstanding season with the booming bats of Harmon Killebrew, Bob Allison, Zoilo Versalles and an outstanding pitching staff headed by Jim Kaat, Jim Perry and Dean Chance. There was every reason to believe the Twins would be strong pennant contenders. Killebrew, a future Hall of Famer and one of the game's most powerful sluggers, led his team to the opening victory.

The fans were in no hurry to leave after the game and plenty still stood outside the stadium when the players and announcers made their way through the crowd to join their families and head for home. Amid all that excitement, I suddenly had a very empty feeling.

I wasn't going home to my family, because my family was still in Milwaukee. I was going to a lonely hotel room.

I was feeling really sorry for myself when I heard a friendly voice behind me say, "Nice game, Harmon!" My spirits soared instantly as I turned to say "Thank you.." Then I saw Harmon Killebrew walking right behind me.

Harmon, Killebrew that is, stopped to give the fan an autograph. Harmon, Merle that is, a bit deflated and depressed, headed for a lonely hotel room.

Making It Okie Dokie In Muskogee

One of the weirdest assignments of my television career took me to a high school gym in Muskogee, Oklahoma, for ABC's Wide World of Sports on a wintry Thursday night in 1971. Our crew had to do a re-take of a basketball game starring Marques Haynes and his Harlem Magicians because the one taped in Baltimore the previous Sunday afternoon lacked one important ingredient.

A crowd.

Haynes and his troupe put on a tremendous show in the big Baltimore arena, but I think there were more camera operators and production people than fans in the place. Roone Arledge, president of ABC Sports and inventor of Wide World of Sports, insisted that every show be pin-point perfect. When that Baltimore tape reached Arledge in New York and he saw no crowd or crowd reaction, he went a little beserk.

"We can't put this on the air!" he screamed. "Find out where Haynes is taking his team next, go there and shoot a new show! And this time be sure there's a full house!"

ABC was determined to show the game on Saturday, because CBS Sports was showing the Harlem Globetrotters the next day and without Marques Haynes the "Globies" didn't have quite the pizazz they had when Haynes was putting on his dazzling dribbling exhibition for them. Now he was doing all that stuff for his own team and his followers and ABC believed it would make a great program for Wide World.

A crowd wouldn't be a problem in Muskogee, because it was scheduled in a high school gym that would be packed. Haynes, a native of Sand Springs, Oklahoma, and former Langston University star, was a hot ticket there. But it really got tough after that.

I arrived in Muskogee at 9 a.m. Thursday and quickly learned the airline had lost my luggage. The only clothes I had was what I was wearing on the flight: hop-sack Levis, chucka boots and a turtle neck sweater. No way I was going on television that night in that outfit. Arledge would not let anyone appear on a Wide World of Sports program without the Wide World blazer, highlighted by the Wide World of Sports pocket patch. To my knowledge, only one person ever appeared on a Wide World show without that pocket patch. Verne Lundquist was doing a show in Moscow and his luggage was lost and there was no time to ship in a blue blazer or pocket patch.

My problem in Muskogee wasn't quite that bad. Producer Chet Forte sent one of his assistants to a men's clothing store to purchase a new outfit and it just so happened someone in the crew, fearing the wrath of Roone, carried an extra Wide World of Sports pocket patch in his briefcase.

But this was nothing in comparison with a huge problem with the arena. Marques Haynes had booked the game into an ancient high school gym with terrible lighting that made it impossible to televise the game there. Not even the genius of director Joe Aceti, one of the most talented in television, could pull it off in that place.

So Forte, Haynes and Aceti huddled and somehow managed to get the game switched to the gym of a sleek new high school. But what about the crowd? How could you switch the site of the game on short notice? You buy every available spot on every radio and TV station in Muskogee and convince the local afternoon newspaper to run special-notice ads calling attention to the new location of the game. It worked. The new location was much larger than the previous one and more tickets were sold. The Harlem Magicians and Tulsa Oilers were ready to rock and roll.

The television production truck had moved to the new site, and the cameras put in place in the gym. The ABC crew and Haynes, along with his key performers, held a production meeting to go over the format, which included comedy as well as skill routines. Some of the special dribbling exhibitions by Haynes and some of the trick shots by Bob "Trick" White would be pre-recorded on tape starting at 7:30 that night with tip-off of the actual "game" at 8 p.m. The game itself would be videotaped in its entirety, then flown to the ABC production center in New York and edited down to fit the allotted time in that Saturday's Wide World show. All of the last-minute changes had been made and by 4 p.m. producer Forte drew a big breath and said, "We did it. We're ready to roll."

But the frenzy had only begun.

Darkness fell on Muskogee early that winter day and lights came on across the city. But when the switches were turned on in the ABC production truck the power surge was more than the transformer in the area could handle. The truck went dark, the gym went dark, and so did hundreds of homes in that section of Muskogee.

How could the terrific ABC crew handle a power blackout? The electric company said it was impossible to restore power in time for the game. They did say they would send out an emergency portable generator but it wouldn't be powerful enough to meet the requirements of the production truck and gym.

"Send it!" Forte screamed. At least the portable generator would provide enough light in the gym for arriving ticket-holders to find their way to their seats. The fans, of course, assumed the game would start on time, never realizing the game probably would be called off. But Forte, Aceti and the ABC crew weren't about to accept "the agony of defeat."

Aceti asked, "Hey, where do they get the power to drill those oil wells we saw along the highway coming into Muskogee? Those things are out in the middle of nowhere and they must require a lot of electricity to do that drilling."

One of the locals who had been hired to pull camera cables said, "Those drilling crews have big generators they haul out to the well site and they're so powerful they could light a small city."

"There's out answer," Forte said. "Let's buy one, rent one or steal one but we have to get one in here immediately."

An oil field supply company was contacted and it said it would be glad to rent us a generator, but most of its work force had gone home for the day. It might take two or three hours to find an operator and a big truck to pull the generator out to the ABC production truck, hook everything up and supply the needed electrical power. And it would be expensive.

"Forget the cost!" Forte yelled. "Get busy! We're going to start shooting at 7:30."

Forte's blood pressure went up some more when 7:30 came and the generator had just arrived. It would be another hour before we could start shooting all the pre-game stuff.

By now the gym was packed with fans and the Harlem Magicians and their opponents had come out on the floor to warm up under the dim light provided by the small portable generator. By 8 p.m. the fans, still sitting in relative darkness, were getting restless. Forte asked me to go to the public address system, explain the delay and plead for patience.

The Magicians continued their workout, and Bob "Trick" White appeased the crowd by making several of his reverse shots from mid-court. I didn't even think he would make the first one. You try it some time. Stand in the center circle facing one basket, lean back and fire the ball to the basket behind you..

The crowd appreciated White's exhibition but soon they started to chant, "Play ball!"

Another 30 minutes passed. The crowd was getting mean. The players were getting impatient, too, but Marques Haynes reprimanded them, reminding them there was sizeable TV money at stake.

Again, Forte asked me to go out on the floor and announce the game would be starting soon. Realizing I had to take one for good old ABC, I went out and was greeted by the loudest boos I had ever heard. Then suddenly the gym exploded with the brightest, and most welcome, lights I had ever seen. The crowd went wild.

Bob "Trick" White moved to center-court for his pet behind-the-back shot. Our tape machines were rolling and the crowd fell silent in suspense. White missed, and the crowd groaned. So did I. Inexplicably, he missed his next nine tries. Haynes came over and told White he'd better give up. The same message came from producer Forte. White, sweating like crazy by now, asked to try one more shot.

The physical and mental strain was being shared by everyone in the gym. I told the crowd over the P.A. system that this would be White's last attempt to make his specialty. In almost stone silence, White bounced the ball several times, then leaned back so far he almost collapsed on the floor. He spun the ball out of his hands toward the basket behind him and *SWISH*! He made it. The crowd went bananas while White collapsed on the floor for a minute or so. Some time after 9 p.m. we finally got the game underway.

The incomparable Haynes and his Magicians gave a magnificent performance and the crowd went home happy. When the game was over, the ABC crew continued to work in the production truck with preliminary edits. Finally, long after midnight, we loaded into vans and drove an hour to the Tulsa airport to catch a 6 a.m. flight to New York. On Friday afternoon the show was edited down to the 30 minutes allotted it on the Wide World of Sports program the next afternoon. The final edit was great and I did the voice layover. Viewers who tuned in Wide World the next day saw a very slick package.

And our crew, proud that we came back from Muskogee with the goods, stretched out for a long nap.

John Wooden's Beloved Assistant Coach

How lucky can a sports announcer get? During my career I had an opportunity to work with not one but two of the legendary coaches in college basketball.

First there was Dr. Forrest C. "Phog" Allen at the University of Kansas in the final years of his illustrious career, prior to his retirement. Two decades later, there was John Wooden, "The Wizard of Westwood" who led UCLA to 10 NCAA championships in 12 years from 1964-75, a feat I dare say never will be matched.

After Coach Wooden's retirement, he signed on with TVS, the independent television network, to be an analyst on several games. TVS had regional networks set up for most of the major conferences and my play-by-play assignment was for Big 10 games each Saturday afternoon. I was fortunate enough to have Wooden on several of the games I covered during the 1976-77 season. Although UCLA and the Pac-10 lay claim to him, Wooden's roots went back to Purdue University in 1930-32 where he was one of the outstanding players in the conference.

At dinner with Coach Wooden and his wife Nell one night before a Saturday telecast, the conversation got around to Nell being quite a fan. She attended all the home games during his UCLA career and sat just a row or two behind the Bruins' bench. I asked the coach if she ever gave him any tips on strategy. Wooden laughed as he related the story of one game which UCLA seemed to be winning quite handily. In the late stages of the contest he decided to have his team go

into a stall to start killing the clock. Wooden said the crowd became rather quite with nothing happening on the floor except his players holding the ball. Suddenly, he recognized a small voice behind him uttering, "too soon, too soon."

He didn't have to look around to see who was offering this critical analysis. He had heard that beautiful soft voice many, many years, from his home state of Indiana to sunny Southern California.

Coach Wooden beamed as he recalled the moment.

"Sure enough, Nell was right," he said. "I had put my team into a stall 'too soon, too soon' and the other team went on a tear. We couldn't regain our momentum and wound up almost losing the game."

Merle and UCLA coaching legend John Wooden worked together on an NCAA Regional telecast from Los Angeles.

The Fan Fair Story

I grew up around my father's neighborhood grocery store in Salem, Illinois, and I made up my mind early in life that I would never be involved in any kind of retail business. I hated it.

So, in the 29th year of my sports broadcasting career, I became a retailer.

I founded Merle Harmon's Fan Fair in 1977, a store which I thought would become a sports fan's delight. And it was. It featured officially licenses merchandise of professional and collegiate teams and we built it in a major regional shopping mall in Milwaukee. The store was the first of its type in America to be located in a high-traffic retail setting. Of course, it didn't hurt that I was broadcasting the

Merle received the Graham McNamee Award, which is given to a sportscaster who has achieved success in a second field of endeavor.

Milwaukee Brewers' baseball games. I also had been the voice of the Milwaukee Braves before the team moved to Atlanta in 1966. I had pretty good exposure in the Milwaukee market and having my name on the Fan Fair store didn't hurt.

The New York Jets deserve some credit for the whole idea. As the Jets' radio announcer, I received a unique Christmas gift from the club one year: a desk lamp with a base made from a Jets helmet. It was a pretty interesting idea, and it wasn't long before anyone who saw it was asking me where they could get one. Of course, none were available anywhere.

When I wore a Milwaukee Brewers cap which the team equipment manager gave me, people asked me, "Where can I get one, the real thing like you're wearing?" The answer was nowhere, unless you knew a player or team executive. Souvenir team caps, T-shirts, pennants and the like were available only at stadium and arena concessions stands. Teams weren't interested in having anyone wear any part of an official uniform. New York Yankees owner George Steinbrenner once was quoted as saying that nobody except team personnel ever would wear any type of authentic cap or any other piece of a Yankee uniform. In later years, millions of dollars of royalties changed his mind.

Years before I took the plunge with Fan Fair, I attended a luncheon in New York hosted by one of the Jets' radio sponsors, Abraham and Strauss department stores. It was prior to the start of the 1965 season and Jets CEO Sonny Werblin had made a huge splash by signing Alabama quarterback Joe Namath to an unheard-off $429,000 contract. Broadway Joe was the biggest thing to hit the Big Apple in pro football history. Many teams hooked onto the team in their advertising. One business ran a large ad featuring a small boy asleep in his bed, dreaming he was Namath, wearing Joe's number 12 uniform jersey.

Bingo! My light bulb went on. At the luncheon I asked the A&S executive if he had seen that ad and he replied that he had. "Then I have a great idea for you," I said. "Manufacture kids pajamas sets and make the top into a replica of Joe Namath's jersey."

He was excited. "Great! You make 'em and I'll put them in all our stores," he said.

"But I'm not a manufacturer," I said. "I don't know anything abut that business."

"We're not manufacturers either; we're retailers," he replied. "You should pursue your idea, though."

I didn't, but I wish I had. The entire sports license product business mushroomed into a $12 billion dollar industry within the next 25 years.

Occasionally I daydreamed about the possibility of putting a business together. I didn't want to manufacture team products, but if someone else did maybe I could open a store that appealed to sports fans who would love to have items with which to identify with their favorite teams.

My thoughts would take me back to when I was a ninth-grader selling magazines door to door to save enough money to take the train to St. Louis, some sixty miles away, to see my beloved Cardinals play. I could do it on a two-dollar budget. Round-trip train fare was one dollar. Streetcar fare from the St. Louis train station to old Sportsman's Park, where the Cardinals played, was 10 cents each way. A bleachers seat cost 25 cents. A hot dog, soft drink and a bag of peanuts took an another 30 cents, which left me 25 cents to buy Cardinal souvenirs. For that quarter I could come home with a small team pennant and a pencil shaped like a baseball bat with the Cardinal logo on it.

Merle and Paul Molitor visit during the young Milwaukee Brewer star's appearance at Merle Harmon's Fan Fair during the 1978 season.

Merle Harmon's Fan Fair in downtown Milwaukee, like his stores across the country, offered a dazzling array of merchandise.

When school started in the fall, I protected that pencil with my life, making sure my friends saw it and asked me where I got it. As a poor kid in the Depression years, that pencil was my status symbol. It was proof that I had been to St. Louis to see a big-league baseball game. The only place you could get the souvenir items I had was at the concession stands at the ballpark. That memory kept re-surfacing in my mind years later when people asked me where they could get a Jets football helmet desk lamp or a real major league baseball cap.

Ten years after my conversation with that New York department store executive, the idea of a full-blown team shop catering to sports fans was still with me. I discussed it with my family and the reaction was, "You're one of the busiest sports announcers in the country, so why don't you stick with what you enjoy and love? Remember, you've always said you hated the retail business since you were a small boy growing up around your father's grocery store." Still, I couldn't get the idea of opening a shop for fans of every team out of my mind.

Around the kitchen table one night in 1976, it was decided we would take the plunge and operate the venture as a family business. I told my family I would not give up radio and TV, and I didn't. My son, Reid, who managed a retail store in Chicago, would come back to Milwaukee to operate our store and I would continue travelling across the country and halfway around the world broadcasting sports events. As the business grew, Reid would be joined by his brothers, Keith and Kyle, and sister, Kara, in the business. My youngest son, Bruce, was like I once had been. He declared that when he finished school there was no way he ever would get involved in the retail business. He didn't. He is a TV cameraman covering network sports events.

The first Merle Harmon's Fan Fair, "The Sports Fan's Gift Shop," opened in late spring of 1977. We picked a Saturday for our big debut because the Brewers were playing a night game and I was able to secure the services of six players to appear at the store throughout the day to sign autographs. To my surprise, almost the whole team showed up at one time or

Merle Harmon's Fan Fair signs decorated new Comiskey Park, the home of the Chicago White Sox.

Merle met plenty of Japanese business leaders like this corporate chairman while visiting Japan in the mid-80's in behalf of his Fan Fair stores.

another, giving us support for which I always will be grateful. Our entire wing of the mall was packed with fans and customers.

Mall security was doubled to direct foot traffic through the corridors and into our store. The place was jammed wall-to-wall with fans who wanted to get a glimpse, handshakes, pictures and autographs from young Brewer stars such as Robin Yount and Paul Molitor and veterans like Sal Bando and Cecil Cooper.

Security set up lines of rope, weaving back and forth in the hallway in front of our store. Fans waited up to two hours just to get into our place. All stores in our wing of the mall received great exposure as the crowd passed their businesses on their way to ours.

An ice cream shop across the hall had terrific sales. While people waited, they enjoyed eating ice cream—so much so that then the day ended the proprietor came over to congratulate me and thank me for bringing so many people to the mall. He said it was the greatest day he ever had at that location. "We sold every scoop of ice cream in the place!" he said. "My cash register was ringing all day. You did a fantastic job of marketing and promotion in bringing the Brewers in. I hope you did as well as we did."

We didn't. Our store was so packed with people all day long that they couldn't see half the merchandise we had to offer. I felt like asking that ice cream store owner if he would like to pay a portion of *our* costs which gave *him* the biggest day in his store's history.

Our gross sales were a little over $300 for the day, about enough to pay the electric bill. But the exposure was great.

Merle Harmon's Fan Fair, through franchising, grew to a chain of 140 stores over the next 17 years. The company was sold in 1996. It was a great ride for a guy who swore he'd never get into the retail business.

Great Day? Not For Me

Remember the hair color for men called Great Day? The product had just been introduced to the public in the late '60's and the advertising agency for Great Day was putting together a campaign to convince men with gray hair—especially those who were prematurely gray—to regain that youthful look with a few easy applications of Great Day lotion to their hair.

The ad agency decided to build a campaign featuring laborers, athletes and businessmen with a "before" and "after" look, demonstrating the impressive darkening of men's hair when they used Great Day. One of the commercials the agency wanted to develop involved Sam Mele, who managed the Minnesota Twins into the 1965 World Series against the Los Angeles Dodgers.

Sam was perfect for the role. He had a full head of salt-and-pepper hair and the looks of a movie star or a construction worker. Take your pick.

Mele was called to New York for a test and quickly was selected to do the commercial. The agency also wanted a sports announcer with enough gray in his hair to participate in the commercial alongside Mele, and I also was brought to New York for the hair test. It was determined that I probably would do, but first the agency had to get Mele under contract.

On my way home that day I already was counting the fees and residuals and wondering what my family would think of my new hair look. I knew they would like it because we needed the money.

But Sam Mele received a different reaction when he walked into his home. His wife and daughters took one look at their leading man with solid black hair and started laughing. That hardly was the reaction he expected. Sam was so perturbed he turned the deal down.

His decision almost cost one of my kids a college education. At least that's what I told him when I tried to get him to reconsider, but it didn't work. It did not turn out to be a "Great Day" for me.

The ad agency scrapped the idea of using television to sell their client's product and went to a print campaign featuring Duke Snider, the old Dodger star who had become the Montreal Expos' broadcaster. Remember the photos of Duke with gray hair on the left side of his head and dark hair on the right? Duke's "Great Day" turned into several years of great residuals.

Seeing Double

The Milwaukee Brewers once had a premier relief pitcher named Tom Murphy, who earlier had been a starter of some renown for the California Angels. As a reliever, Tom grew into one of the Brewers' most valuable properties in 1974 when he appeared in 70 games, saving 20 and winning 10 more.

Brewers owner Bud Selig would do just about anything for one of his players as long as it didn't cost too much money. He liked to visit with his players, was interested in their families and enjoyed a positive relationship with them. Tom Murphy was one of the highest-paid Brewers and a big crowd favorite because he frequently sauntered in from the bullpen and stopped the opposition cold.

Tom was a lanky, 6-foot-3 185-pounder who had the looks of a Hollywood movie star. He also had an identical twin named Roger. I mean, they were dead ringers of each other. Same voices, same mannerisms, same big smiles.

They had a lot of fun when Tom pitched for the Angels. Roger occasionally would don one of Tom's uniforms, stroll out on the field during batting practice and shag a few fly balls in the outfield. Sometimes he would do an interview with an unsuspecting out-of-town reporter or broadcaster. The guys who covered the Angels regularly usually were in on the scam, as were some of the Angel players who gathered around to listen to the interviews. They got a big laugh from some of the answers Roger/Tom gave the unsuspecting reporter.

After Tom joined the Brewers, Roger visited him in the clubhouse and the sight of them together astonished Tom's new teammates, who didn't know he had an identical twin. This inspired them to have some fun with the kind, soft-spoken Selig.

Roger put on one of Tom's uniforms and, with his brother and several other players in his wake, marched from the clubhouse up to the Brewer general offices. While the others huddled in a private hallway within earshot of Selig's office, Roger, as Tom, told Selig's secretary that he wanted to see the boss. He immediately was ushered into the owner's private office.

"Tommy, it's great to see you!" Selig said, pumping Roger's hand. "Man, you're doing a wonderful job and I surely do appreciate it. Grab a chair and tell me what I can do for you."

With that, Roger plopped into a big comfortable chair, put his feet up on Selig's desk and, feigning anger, said. "I'll tell you what you can do for me! I want a salary increase double what you're paying me now or I'm going home to California."

Selig was in shock. He never had been approached by one of his players this way.

"But, Tommy," he said, "you're already one of the highest paid players in the American League. I thought you were very happy with what we're paying you."

Roger shrugged off Selig's appeasing words and continued to pour it on while the owner sat there open-mouthed.

Finally, the real Tom Murphy and his teammates couldn't hold back any longer as they listened outside Selig's door. They laughed so loud that Selig got up from his desk and opened the door to see what was going on. He found himself staring in the face of the real Tom Murphy.

Selig did a double-take, looked at the guy sitting in his office, and was totally confused.

Then Tom introduced Selig to his identical twin, Roger, and they all share a good laugh.

"Roger," Selig said, "you look like Tom, you talk like Tom, and you act like Tom. Now, if you can only pitch like Tom, I'll pay you a salary like Tom's.

How It All Began

I had been in sportscasting for many years before I learned just how and when my profession got its start. One day I found material in my library on some early sportscasters like Bill Stern, Ted Husing and Graham McNamee. I was so absorbed I spent most of the day reading how it all began.

In April of 1921, Johnny Ray and Johnny Dundee were scheduled for a light heavyweight boxing match in Pittsburgh. There was one of those new-fangled "wireless" broadcasting stations in Pittsburgh and it was struggling for any kind of recognition at the time. Its call letters were KDKA, which today is one of the great stations in America.

But back in 1921, it was nothing until someone had the bright idea of broadcasting that fight and persuaded a popular Pittsburgh sports writer, Florent Gibson, to deliver the blow-by-blow description. According to KDKA history that was the first *live* broadcast of a sports event anywhere.

Later that year, KDKA staff announcer Harold Arlin did the first broadcast of a baseball game, between the Pirates and Philadelphia Phillies. Before the year ended, Arlin did the first football broadcast when he described the game between the University of West Virginia and the University of Pittsburgh. Coverage of sports events on radio was growing.

By 1923, radio and sports had found themselves quite compatible. The marriage went big-time and McNamee became the first high-profile sportscaster. He broadcast the World Series that October and in late November he called the Army-Navy football game.

McNamee became the father of the true sportscasting profession. Since there was no one he might pattern himself after, he developed his own style and technique. He was radio's first big star. He was hired by a fledgling network, NBC, and covered everything from political conventions to opera in addition to his sportscasting duties.

On New Year's Day 1927, NBC had McNamee in Pasadena, California, to cover the Rose Bowl game between Stanford and Alabama. It was the first coast-to-coast broadcast, and radio became truly national in scope.

CBS wasn't about to let NBC run away with everything so that network hired a young man with a well-modulated voice, perfect diction and what was sometimes described acid tongue to take on McNamee and NBC. His name was Ted Husing and, with apologies to Howard Cosell, he was the first sports announcer "to tell it like it is."

Husing quickly attracted a large national following with his candor but he also collected a lot of enemies in the process. His description of a Harvard halfback's performance as "putrid" got him barred from Harvard broadcasts. The president of CBS had to call the president of Harvard to get Husing reinstated. Husing's broadcast of the 1934 World Series between the St. Louis Cardinals and Detroit Tigers resulted in baseball commissioner Judge Kennesaw Mountain Landis banning him from future World Series. All Husing did was call the umpires "inadequate."

In retrospect, it seems the commissioner overreacted but he may have been a little fatigued by the time he dealt with Husing. It was a tough Series all the way around for Judge Landis.

He had to put up with the Cardinals' outlandish, flamboyant star pitcher, Jerome Herman "Dizzy" Dean. Dean hurled every insult he could think of at the Tigers. On the mound, he would look scornfully at a batter, tell him what pitch he was going to throw and then challenge him to hit it. One rarely did. Soon the Tigers were steaming and lost their concentration, which was exactly what Dean wanted.

In the ninth inning of the seventh and deciding game in Detroit, Dizzy was on the mound with an 11-0 lead when the normally fearsome Tiger slugger, Hank Greenberg, came to bat. As Greenberg dug in, Dizzy yelled, "Hey, Hank, ain't you fellers got no pinch hitters?"

Those Gashouse Gang Cardinals heckled Tiger players and Tiger fans. When Joe Medwick roared into third baseman Marv Owen with spikes high in the sixth inning of the final game, Owen retaliated by challenging Medwick to fisticuffs. That suited Medwick just fine, but umpires stepped in and quickly restored peace. But when Medwick went out to his left field position in the bottom of the inning, Tiger fans in the left field seats unloaded on him. They threw everything they could get their hands on, littering the field with apples, oranges and beer bottles.

Judge Landis stopped the game, called Cardinal manager Frankie Frisch and Medwick over to his box and announced he was removing Medwick from the game for his own safety. It was the only time a commissioner has ever thrown a player out of a game. He did it just in time, too. Angry Tiger fans were trying to climb out of the left field stands and come after Medwick.

After Husing described all of this to his national audience in his unique style, perhaps he didn't mind that Judge Landis banned him from broadcasting the World Series again. He already had seen it all—and told it like it was.

Hondo Ate Like He Hit—Big

Over the years, lots of people have asked me to name my favorite sports personality. That's not easy to answer. I really can't pin-point one, so I'll tell you about one of my favorites—a guy called Hondo.

That's Frank Howard, aka The Gentle Giant.

I'm not sure where his nickname of Hondo started. Possibly it came from the movie of the same name which starred John Wayne, a giant of a man, who always portrayed rugged characters who turned out to be good guys. Wayne also was quite an athlete, once a lineman on some top USC football teams under his real name, Marion "Duke" Morrison.

Frank Howard also is a giant of a man, standing 6-7 and weighing in from 260 to 330 pounds during a 40-year major league baseball career as player, coach and manager. And like Wayne, Howard was a rugged college athlete, starring in basketball and baseball at Ohio State. In 1958, he chose baseball over basketball as a professional career for obvious reasons. The Los Angeles Dodgers paid him a $107,000 signing bonus at a time when a college star going into the NBA could expect no more than $50,000.

Howard began his professional career in Victoria, Texas, a Dodger farm club, and soon word reached the Dodger home office that he was smashing mostrous home runs. He was called the strongest man ever to swing a baseball bat. When he sent a line drive whistling back at a pitcher's ear, the pitcher thanked his lucky stars that the ball didn't nail him in the head.

Hondo came up to the Dodgers in 1958 when the team was playing in the Los Angeles Coliseum while their new stadium was being built in Chavez Ravine. The best they could do in creating a baseball field in a football stadium was to hang a 42-foot-high screen as a left field barrier which was only 250 feet from home plate. When Hondo slammed a ball into the screen, fans had to be ready to protect themselves in case the screen didn't stop his blast. And when his smashes cleared the screen, which was often, the fans turned to see if the ball would sail completely out of the huge Coliseum.

Hondo flourished in Chavez Ravine when the Dodgers opened their new stadium in 1961 but he exploded to new heights after a trade to Washington in 1965. Of his 382 career homers in 16 seasons, he hit 136 of them in 1968-70—44, 48 and 44. Fans everywhere loved The Gentle Giant because he loved the fans. I have never met an athlete who was a more humble, friendly, articulate and downright honorable human being than Frank Howard.

He never turned away an autograph seeker and he even thanked the fan for asking. He addressed men as "sir"and women as "ma'am." He was absolutely marvelous with little kids and young people. He encouraged everyone to give their best and strive to succeed regardless of their backgound for he himself had come from one of the very poorest sections of Columbus, Ohio. He knew what it was like to have to work after school to help his family buy groceries and other necessities of life.

God must smile every day at what Frank Howard does for his fellow man. So you can see why he is one of my favorite sports personalities. He also is my friend . . . and, boy, can he eat!

When I was a broadcaster for the Milwaukee Brewers in the 1970's, Frank was one of the Brewer coaches. I loved to talk baseball with him and I especially liked to watch him eat. I mean, he really could put away the groceries.

When the Brewers went to Anaheim to play the California Angels, the team stayed at a hotel close to Disneyland. A mile or so away was a restaurant named Belile. It was one of the few restaurants that was open after night games and I went there often. It was unforgettable. This place served the largest portions of food I had ever seen, and the desserts were huge.

An order of strawberry shortcake covered a large dinner plate. If you ordered a glass of milk, it came in a

16-ounce glass filled to the brim. Coffee was placed on your table in a huge pot with Paul Bunyan-size mugs. A cinnamon roll was the size of the full baking pan. Few people ever could eat everything they ordered.

There was a special breakfast on the menu that always intrigued me. First of all, the price was $15—by today's prices it probably would be at least $25. I knew just the guy to challenge that breakfast. Hondo Howard.

One night after a game in Anaheim, I asked him if he would join me for breakfast the next morning. "Why, I'd love to!" he responded with a booming voice from that huge body. "There are two conditions," I told him. "I get to pick the place and I get to order for you."

"Well, that sounds interesting," he said. "I always enjoy a surprise or two."

We met in the lobby the next morning, hailed a cab and headed for the restaurant. Belile looked like it had been a private home at one time and later turned into a restaurant. Simple, painted signs on the windows called attention to their specials. Once we were seated, the waitress brought us menus but I told her they weren't needed. I ordered bacon, eggs and toast and told the waitress, "Bring my friend your super colossal breakfast.."

"Boy, I can't wait to see this," Hondo said. He soon began to learn what "super colossal" meant.

The waitress served me a glass of orange juice, but brought him a full pitcher. I got a regular pot of coffee, he got a 12-cup pot. Next he ate a large bowl of oatmeal with one of those monster cinnamon rolls, scarfing both down with ease. Six huge pancakes were next, followed by a king-sized platter loaded down with a dozen eggs over easy, six sausage patties, two huge slices of sugar-cured ham, eight thick slices of bacon, four jumbo biscuits floating in country gravy, and a large bowl of fresh mixed fruit.

Hondo grinned at the spread in front of him and announced, "I believe I can handle this." Then he proceeded to wipe out everything. And he never flagged. As he finished his 12th cup of coffee he said, "*BO-OWY!* That was good! Now, what are we having for dessert?"

Gray Matter In The Wild Blue Yonder

Not many college football media guides list the grade point averages of their athletes. A few such as Rice, Vanderbilt and Air Force do. It's not unusual to see 3.7's and 3.9's playing defensive tackle or wide receiver at these schools.

Many have questioned whether schools with such demanding academic standards can produce winning teams with any consistency. Air Force has been able to accomplish that.

Some years ago I attended a sports luncheon where the featured speaker was Air Force football coach Ben Martin. I spent some time with the coach after the luncheon and our talk turned to the cadets' limited practice time because of their heavy academic schedule.

"How long do you have with them each day?" I asked. I was astonished by his answer.

"Well, after they're in uniform and hit the practice field, I have them for about 45 minutes a day," Martin said. "Of course, some of them can't practice every day because of work in the labs."

"How in the world can you develop a winning football team when you can only practice your players 45 minutes a day?" I asked.

His answer was a beauty. "My guys can remember the plays," Ben Martin said.

The Impossible Dream

The year was 1967 and one of the songs that topped the charts week after week was *The Impossible Dream*. It also was the year Dick Williams became manager of the Boston Red Sox, who had finished ninth in the 10-team American League the previous season.

Williams was a fun-loving but hard-nosed outfielder-infielder during his playing career, which began with the Brooklyn Dodgers. He was one of the brightest prospects in the Dodger organization but his career all but ended when he crashed into the outfield wall at Ebbets Field, severely injuring his shoulder and costing him a rifle throwing arm. But Dick had the heart of a lion. He learned to throw with a different motion and went on to spend 13 years in the major leagues with five different teams. He closed out his playing career in 1964 with the Red Sox, who were so impressed with his knowledge of the game and great leadership that they asked to stay in their organization as a minor league manager. Two years later, they promoted him to the big club.

Red Sox players expected Dick to be the same type of personality as a manager that he was as a player, a fun-loving cut-up in the dugout who rode the opposition unmercifully and would do anything to beat the other guy. Many of them were his teammates just two years earlier.

The Red Sox were known as a group of players who were pampered and overpaid by a very generous owner, Tom Yawkey. A Yankee player once said, "Those guys never bleed when they lose. They're a tough team to manage because of their poor attitudes."

Dick Williams quickly changed that when he took over. Even before spring training ended, many his players were complaining he was a tyrant and not the same guy they knew as a player.

Williams established who was running the team, and suddenly the Red Sox were executing the fundamentals and playing heads-up ball, something they hadn't done for several years. They started winning and the Red Sox faithful jammed Fenway Park. And the more they won, the harder Williams drove them. If anybody complained, he was given a seat in the dugout.

The new manager's tactics paid off. A 10-game winning streak in mid-July shot the Red Sox into the middle of a torrid four-team pennant race and it was not decided until the last day of the season.

Three teams still had a chance to win it that final Sunday: the Minnesota Twins, the Detroit Tigers and the Red Sox. The Twins entered that last weekend with the best shot. They held a one-game lead over the Tigers and Red Sox going into the Saturday game at Boston and had ace lefthander Jim Kaat pitching. Kaat was untouchable in the early innings as the Twins took the lead, but then catastrophe struck. Kaat broke a bone in his pitching arm throwing a curve ball and the Red Sox bats came alive against his successor.

Led by the booming bat of Carl Yastrzemski, Boston beat the Twins and tied them for first place. It was the latest in a chain of superb performances by Yastrzemski.

"For the month of September," Ted Williams said, "Yaz was the greatest player who ever lived." That was the supreme compliment for Yaz, especially coming from the man he succeeded in left field for the Red Sox.

So it came down to the final game. If the Red Sox won, they would clinch at least a tie for the pennant because out in Detroit the Tigers were playing the California Angels in a double-header. If the Tigers won both games, they would finish in a tie with the winner of the Minnesota-Boston game, forcing a one-game playoff to determine the American League champion who would play in the World Series.

Boston was crazy with pennant fever. Fenway Park was sold out and ticket scalpers were having a field day. Thousands of fans who had no hope of getting a ticket jammed the streets outside the ballpark, carrying portable radios to hear the game broadcast. They were certain the Red Sox were going to win and they wanted to in be in on the celebration, even if they were outside Fenway Park.

The Red Sox didn't need long to take control of the game, shelling the Twins' starting pitcher, 20-game winner Dean Chance. The game was a runaway. Jim Lonborg, the ace Red Sox righthander and a 20-game winner himself, silenced the Twins' heavy bats and Boston's "Impossible Dream" became a reality. But the race still wasn't over.

In Detroit, the Tigers won the first game of their double-header with the Angels and the second game now was in progress. At Fenway Park, the Red Sox enjoyed a short celebration on the field and then hurried into their clubhouse to gather around radio and TV sets to follow the final game in Detroit.

Within the next hour, the Angels became the darlings of Boston. They won that second game and put the Red Sox in the World Series. A wild celebration erupted across New England.

But it was a heart-breaking setback for the Minnesota Twins—and me.

It was my first year as a Twins announcer and, naturally, I wanted them to win. But I always prided myself in being fair when I called a game, giving full credit when the opponents played well. I wanted to be objective in my reporting, but I was concerned that I might have shown my disappointment in the Twins' Saturday and Sunday losses costing them the pennant. I received my answer to that about a week later in a letter from a Twins fan.

"We thought you were for the Twins all season," the fan wrote, "but in those two games with Red Sox, and especially the final one, you sounded as excited when the Red Sox made big plays as you did when the Twins made big plays."

I appreciated that criticism. I knew I had done my job properly.

About The Authors

Merle Harmon drew plenty of memorable assignments during his 45 years in sports broadcasting but the one on the night of August 8, 1974, was unique. He went into the booth to call a World Football League game and became the only sports announcer in history to introduce the President of the United States for a speech on national television.

With the start of the game on hold, the camera then moved to the White House Oval Office, where a grim Richard Nixon informed the nation that he was resigning the next day. "After that, our game was pretty anti-climactic," Merle said.

Merle Harmon

But much of his far-ranging career certainly wasn't. He broadcast three no-hitters and two perfect major league baseball games, the New York Jets' stunning upset of the Baltimore Colts in Super Bowl III, and Nolan Ryan's 5,000th strikeout. He also got into a beef with the Soviet KGB over some Moscow tourist scenes he shot with his personal camera while covering the World Games. It ended in a draw. The KGB got the film and Merle got to go home.

Always eager for his next assignment, he left Moscow on a Saturday at 9 a.m. and broadcast a baseball game in Minnesota that night. That was life with this man for all seasons. The *Los Angeles Times* called him "a solid professional in every respect", and *TV Guide* wrote "he might be the best radio football play-by-play man ever."

In 1977, Merle added a second career. He founded Merle Harmon's Fan Fair, a national chain of retail stores specializing in the sale of licensed sports merchandise. He sold the company in 1996.

The American Sportscasters Association honored him at their 1993 Hall of Fame Dinner in New York City, presenting him the Graham McNamee Award given to a sportscaster who has achieved success in a second field of endeavor. Previous recipients include President Ronald Reagan, Walter Cronkite, Bryant Gumbel and Larry King. In 1996, Merle was inducted into the Texas Baseball Hall of Fame.

Merle holds degrees from the University of Denver and Graceland College in Iowa. He serves on the Board of Trustees of Graceland and on the Board of Directors of Skillpath Seminars. He formerly served on the Board of the Center of Professional Selling at Baylor University.

Merle and his wife, Jeanette, are the parents of four sons and one daughter and have six grandchildren. They live in Arlington, Texas.

HIS CAREER HIGHLIGHTS:

1949–Graduated from the University of Denver, BA in Radio.

1949-52–Topeka, Kansas. Radio play-by-play minor league baseball, high school and college football and basketball.

1952-54–Lawrence, Kansas. Play-by-play University of Kansas football, basketball and Kansas Relays, track and field on KU Network.

1954–Kansas City. Play-by-play baseball Kansas City Blues of American Association, University of Kansas football and baseball.

1954-61–Kansas City. Play-by-play major league baseball Kansas City A's, college football and basketball.

1961–ABC Television, All Pro Scoreboard.

1962-63–ABC Television, All Pro Scoreboard, Saturday Night Sports and various other assignments.

1963–Kansas City Chiefs radio play-by-play.

1964-72–New York Jets radio play-by-play. ABC Television, College Football Scoreboard, NCAA football play-by-play and other feature assignments.

1964-65–Milwaukee Braves radio play-by-play.

1964-66–Marquette University basketball radio play-by-play.

1967-69–Minnesota Twins radio and television play-by-play. TVS Television Network college basketball play-by-play.

1970-79–Milwaukee Brewers radio play-by-play. TVS college basketball play-by-play.

1973–World Games from Moscow, TVS, anchor.
1974-75–TVS World Football Leaague play-by-play.
1974-76–Big Ten Football Game of the Week play-by-play, KABC, Los Angeles.
1977-1984–NBC Television, play-by-play on NFL, NCAA basketball, major league baseball, Sportsworld and other assignments.
1982-89–Texas Rangers television play-by-play.
1990-94–Special sports events, free lance.
1995–Retired from broadcasting.

Sam Blair began his career as a writer and columnist for *The Dallas Morning News* in October 1954. He retired from the newspaper in December 1995 to develop a variety of creative projects.

"This move is consistent with my policy of changing jobs every 41 years," he said.

During his career with *The News*, Sam wrote on subjects ranging from the Olympic Games to the Oklahoma City bombing, from the Roger Staubach-to-Drew Pearson Hail Mary pass at Minnesota to Texan James Earl Rudder leading his Rangers up the cliffs at Pointe de Hoc for the first battle of D-Day, from heavyweight humorist George Foreman to modern jazz legend Stan Kenton. He also has been active as a free-lance writer, authoring nine books and hundreds of magazine articles.

Sam Blair

Sam has joined his wife, former *Dallas Morning News* White House correspondent Karen Klinefelter, in Blair Productions, a multi-media operation in writing, speaking, publishing, promotions and marketing, working together on some projects and independently on others. They also will consider occasional engagements as ballroom dancers.

"This is a great opportunity to create and have some more fun," Sam said.

Sam and Karen are natives of Dallas. They moved back to their hometown in 1993 from Arlington, where they had lived since 1985. Both graduated from the University of Texas at Austin, as did their sons, Jason and Collin.

OTHER BOOKS BY SAM BLAIR:

Dallas Cowboys: Pro or Con? (Doubleday), 1970.
Staubach: First Down, Lifetime To Go, with Roger Staubach and Bob St. John, (Word), 1974.
Grant Teaff: I Believe, with Grant Teaff (Word), 1975.
Earl Campbell: The Driving Force (Word), 1980.
Super Mex, with Lee Trevino (Random House), 1983.
Bob Lilly Reflections, with Bob Lilly (Lilly-Blair), 1983.
The Snake in The Sandtrap, with Lee Trevino (Henry Holt), 1985.
Aggies Handbook (Anecdotal History of Texas A&M Football) (Midwest Sports Publications), 1996.
Note: For information on ordering *Bob Lilly Reflections* and *Aggies Handbook* by mail, call 1-800-545-5961.

For information about ordering
Merle Harmon Stories
by mail, call 1-800-995-6656